KINGSHIP IN NORTHERN INDIA

(*CIR. 600 A.D.—1200 A.D.*)

Ram Charitra Prasad Singh
Patna University, Patna

MOTILAL BANARSIDASS
DELHI :: VARANASI :: PATNA

BUNGALOW ROAD, JAWAHARNAGAR, DELHI-7
CHOWK, VARANASI (U.P.)
ASHOK RAJ PATH, PATNA (BIHAR)

First Edition 1968
Price R

Printed in India by Shantilal Jain, at Shri Jainendra Press, Bungalow Road, Jawaharnagar, Delhi-7, and published by Sundarlal Jain, Motilal Banarsidass, Bungalow Road, Jawahar Nagar, Delhi-7

PREFACE

A distinctive feature of the political organisation of Northern India in post-Gupta times is the emergence of centrifugal forces. The country was divided into several kingdoms, each trying to gain at the cost of others. Muslims took advantage of it and succeeded in snatching away the Indian sovereignty.

We can better understand the situation if we examine the type of kingship in early mediaeval period. The book begins with a review of the different sources that were used in course of our study, and in the following chapter attempts have been made to explain the concept of kingship. A comparison between Indian concept and Roman concept of kingship as shown in Dante has been attempted. It is followed by an exposition of Magical and Divine Origin of Kingship. An analysis of the available materials shows that the Divinity of the king was both claimed and recognised by the Indians of our period. The book also shows how the rulers of the period possessed political, social, religious, judicial and military powers in their kingdoms. These characteristics of Indian kings remind us of the absolute monarch of Aristotle. It seems that numerous duties were assigned to the king but their performance depended on the personality of the king. There was, however, no effective check upon the negligent king. The ultimate ownership of land is treated in some detail and on the evidence of literary, epigraphic and foreign accounts it has been suggested that the king was looked on as the owner of the soil. The book also deals with the diplomatic organisations and the policy of peace. In conclusion we compare Indian kingship with the Islamic and consider its contribution to the weak resistance of the Hindus to the Muslim invaders.

The book is based on a thesis submitted and approved for the degree of the Doctor of Philosophy in the University of London in 1957 but it has been made up-to-date.

In the preparation of the work I owe most sincere gratitude to my teacher Prof. A.L. Basham for his able supervision. A kinder and more helpful teacher than he can hardly be met. I express my sincere gratitude to Prof. R.S. Sharma of the Patna University who made several valuable suggestions in the preparation of the book. I am thankful to Prof. A.K. Narain of the Hindu University and Dr. A.H. Dani of the Dacca University for their valuable comments. My thanks are also due to Dr. D.N. Jha, Shri P.N. Sahay of the Patna University who offered their help in the last stage of the preparation of the book. Finally, I would like to thank the librarians and other members of the libraries of School of Oriental and African Studies, London University, India Office Library, London, and the Library of the Bihar Research Society, Patna, who offered every possible help to me.

R.C. Prasad Singh.

ABBREVIATIONS

Āca.	Ācārāṅga Sūtra.
A.C.	Antiquities of Chamba, J.Ph. Vogel.
Agni	Agni Purāṇa.
A.S.A.I.	The Argarian System in Ancient India, U.N. Ghoshal.
Ait. Br.	Aitareya Brāhmaṇa.
Apa.	Aparājitapṛcchā of Bhuvanadeva
A.H.P.	Some Aspects of Hindu Polity, D. R. Bhandarkar.
Arthaśāstra	Kauṭilīya Arthaśāstra.
Bṛh. Ar.	Bṛhaspati Arthaśāstra.
Bṛha.	Bṛhaspati Smṛti.
B.S.O.A.S.	Bulletin of the School of Oriental and African Studies.
C.R.	Campū Rāmāyaṇa of King Bhoja.
E.I.	Epigraphia Indica.
Gautama	Gautama Smṛti.
H.A.I.	Hindu Administrative Institutions, V.R.R. Dikshitar.
H.C.	Harṣacaritam of Bāṇa.
H.D.S.	History of Dharmaśāstra, P.V. Kane.
H M.	Hammira Mahākāvya of Nayacandra.
H.P.	Harivaṃśa Purāṇa of Jinasena Sūri.
I.A.	Indian Antiquary.
I.H.Q.	Indian Historical Quarterly.
J.A.O.S.	Journal of the American Oriental Society.
J.D.L.	Journal of the Department of Letters Calcutta University.
J.R.A.S.	Journal of the Royal Asiatic Society.
Kām.	Kāmandakīyanītisāra.
Kāt.	Kātyāyana Smṛti.
Kṛtyakalpa	Kṛtyakalpataru of Lakṣmīdhara.
M.P.	Mahā Purāṇa.
Mān.	Mānasollāsa of Someśvara.
Manu	Manu Smṛti.

Mārk.	Mārkaṇḍeya Purāṇa.
Mat.	Matsya Purāṇa.
Monarchy	Monarchy and Three Political Letters of Dante, tr. D. Nicholl.
Nārada	Nārada Smṛti.
N.I.	Northern India.
N.V.	Nītivākyāmṛta of Somadeva Sūri.
P.C.	Prabandha Cintāmaṇi of Merutuṅgācārya.
P.R.	Pṛthvīrāj Rāso.
R.C.	Rāmacaritam of Sandhyākaranandin.
Rāj.	Rājataraṅgiṇī of Kalhaṇa.
R.N.	Rājanītiratnākara of Caṇḍeśvara.
S.B.E.	Sacred Books of the East.
S.G.A.I.	State and Government in Ancient India, by A.S. Altekar.
Śukra	Śukranītisāra.
S.S. or Sūtra	Suvarṇabhāsottama Sūtra.
U.R.C.	Uttara-Rāma-Caritam of Bhavabhūti.
Vaśiṣṭha	Vaśiṣṭha Smṛti.
Yāj.	Yājñavalkya Smṛti.

ABBREVIATIONS

Āca.	Ācārāṅga Sūtra.
A.C.	Antiquities of Chamba, J.Ph. Vogel.
Agni	Agni Purāṇa.
A.S.A.I.	The Argarian System in Ancient India, U.N. Ghoshal.
Ait. Br.	Aitareya Brāhmaṇa.
Apa.	Aparājitapṛcchā of Bhuvanadeva
A.H.P.	Some Aspects of Hindu Polity, D. R. Bhandarkar.
Arthaśāstra	Kauṭilīya Arthaśāstra.
Bṛh. Ar.	Bṛhaspati Arthaśāstra.
Bṛha.	Bṛhaspati Smṛti.
B.S.O.A.S.	Bulletin of the School of Oriental and African Studies.
C.R.	Campū Rāmāyaṇa of King Bhoja.
E.I.	Epigraphia Indica.
Gautama	Gautama Smṛti.
H.A.I.	Hindu Administrative Institutions, V.R.R. Dikshitar.
H.C.	Harṣacaritam of Bāṇa.
H.D.S.	History of Dharmaśāstra, P.V. Kane.
H M.	Hammira Mahākāvya of Nayacandra.
H.P.	Harivaṃśa Purāṇa of Jinasena Sūri.
I.A.	Indian Antiquary.
I.H.Q.	Indian Historical Quarterly.
J.A.O.S.	Journal of the American Oriental Society.
J.D.L.	Journal of the Department of Letters Calcutta University.
J.R.A.S.	Journal of the Royal Asiatic Society.
Kām.	Kāmandakīyanītisāra.
Kāt.	Kātyāyana Smṛti.
Kṛtyakalpa	Kṛtyakalpataru of Lakṣmīdhara.
M.P.	Mahā Purāṇa.
Mān.	Mānasollāsa of Someśvara.
Manu	Manu Smṛti.

Mārk.	Mārkaṇḍeya Purāṇa.
Mat.	Matsya Purāṇa.
Monarchy	Monarchy and Three Political Letters of Dante, tr. D. Nicholl.
Nārada	Nārada Smṛti.
N.I.	Northern India.
N.V.	Nītivākyāmṛta of Somadeva Sūri.
P.C.	Prabandha Cintāmaṇi of Merutuṅgācārya.
P.R.	Pṛthvīrāj Rāso.
R.C.	Rāmacaritam of Sandhyākaranandin.
Rāj.	Rājataraṅgiṇī of Kalhaṇa.
R.N.	Rājanītiratnākara of Caṇḍeśvara.
S.B.E.	Sacred Books of the East.
S.G.A.I.	State and Government in Ancient India, by A.S. Altekar.
Śukra	Śukranītisāra.
S.S. or Sūtra	Suvarṇabhāsottama Sūtra.
U.R.C.	Uttara-Rāma-Caritam of Bhavabhūti.
Vaśiṣṭha	Vaśiṣṭha Smṛti.
Yāj.	Yājñavalkya Smṛti.

CONTENTS

Chapter I
INTRODUCTION

Most historians of Hindu India have concentrated their studies on ancient history and political thought, and very little has been said about the political thought of the early mediaeval period, a period which marks the end of Hindu sovereignty in Northern India.

Several texts on political theory, which setting out the rules of statecraft to be followed by kings, have survived from this time. We shall consider the chief of these in what appears to us to be their order of importance for our subject.

The *Śukranītisāra* is the most important source of this period. The book is divided into five chapters, of which the most important is the fourth, with seven sections treating the characteristics of friends, treasury, princely education, social customs, royal functions, fortresses and the royal army. The three earlier chapters deal with the duties of the princes, the function of the king and his officers, and general rules of morality. The fifth chapter is a collection of various verses on morality and statecraft and probably an addition.

The detailed analysis and division of the subject suggest that Śukra had a very complicated form of government in his view. He advised the king to maintain friendly relation with other kings[1] and did not go into the details of the doctrines of *maṇḍala* usually found in the works of this kind. He laid down a daily routine for the king and advised the king to abide by the well thought out plans of his counsellors, office bearers and subjects. But as far as we can see most rulers of this period paid very little attention to the advice of text books such as this, and writers on politics were rather theoreticians than practical politicians like the author of the *Arthaśastra*. The text of Śukra, as we have it, is certainly later than our period, since it refers to fire arms, but the main body of the work was probably written in twelfth century A.D.[2] In his discussion of administration

1. *Śukra*, iv. section I, ver. 73-74.
2. *S. G. A. I.*, p. 11.

Śukra shows some originality, but most of what he says about kingship can be found in older sources.

The *Nīti-vākyamṛta* of Somadeva Sūri is one of the most important *nīti* texts of the period in question. Like several others, the author deals with various aspects of Indian polity, such as the different constituents of kingship, princely education, and rules for royal administration. Its author was a Jaina, but his works show little difference of approach from the similar texts written by Hindus. The work is dated[1] in the 10th century A.D., and appears to be more closely related to the *Kāmandaka-nītisāra* than to other texts.

Next comes the *Kāmandakanītisāra*, which is probably somewhat earlier than our period, and may be dated[2] in A.D. 400-600. Since it has very often been quoted by the authors of our period and since the present study includes the 6th century A.D. it would not be reasonable to ignore it on the ground that the text belongs to an early period. The book is divided into nineteen sections. The first chapter deals with the king, his duties and dangers. Chapter two presents an account of the royal education, chapter four enumerates the seven constituents of kingship; chapter six shows how the thorns of kingship should be weeded out. Chapter seven deals with the king's reactions with the royal family. Chapter eight gives advice on his relations with other kings, the formation of the *maṇḍala* and the different ways of avoiding war. Chapter eleven tells how a king should hold counsel with his ministers, and chapter twelve presents rules regarding the envoys and spies. Other chapters deal with topics with which we are not at present concerned.

In the beginning of the book Kāmandaka[3] admits that his views are in harmony with the views of those who are well versed in the science of politics. The book in fact appears to be a summary of parts of Kauṭilya's *Arthaśāstra*. But there is a great difference between the two works. Kauṭilya's *Arthaśāstra* is a practical manual of government probably of Mauryan times, while the book in question reduces the advice of the old text to a set of theoretical rules recommended for Indian kings.

1. *S. G. A. I.*, p. 10.
2. H. D. S., vol. III, p. xviii.
3. *Kām.*, ch. 1, ver. 8.

Two further important works of the period are the *Rāja-dharmakāṇḍa* of the *Kṛtyakalpataru* by Lakṣmīdhara and the *Rāja-nītiratnākara* of Caṇḍeśvara. Lakṣmīdhara is described as a counsellor of the twelfth century Gāhaḍavāla king Govindacandra.[1] Therefore, it is quite possible that the ideals of kingship depicted in the *Kṛtyakalpataru* were popular in the Gāhaḍavāla kingdom. Lakṣmīdhara does not say anything of his own in the text, and the same is the case with Caṇḍeśvara, who is thought to belong to the 13th century A.D. Both writers merely quote passages from Manu, Yājñavalkya and other law books, and comment on a few words or phrases.[2] The *Kāmandakanītisāra*, the *Matsya*, the *Markaṇḍeya*, the *Viṣṇu*, the *Agni* and several other *Purāṇas* are also quoted very frequently. Thus the political views held by these two authors are the same as those propounded by the ancient sages.

Next comes the *Yuktikalpataru* of king Bhoja of Dhāra. It is described by the author as compiled from the *nibandhas* of various ancient sages who wrote on the subject. The work contains not only theoretical precepts but also practical advice on such topics as the training of horses for army and building of ships for navy. As the author himself admits, the matter on kingship has little of any originality.

Next comes the *Bṛhaspati Arthaśāstra*. It is written in the *Sūtra* style, and no commentary to it has yet been found. The *nīti* is addressed to Indra, the king of the Gods. The text states that there is only one science for king, and that is *daṇḍanīti*. According to it the king is advised to be tolerant, considerate, etc., and economical in his expenditures. A daily time table is provided for the king, and its adherance to a regular programme is recommended. Finally, the book, demands a high standard of morality of the king. The text says little if anything that is not to be found in earlier texts.

There is some importance for our purpose in the works of two commentators of the period, Medhātithi and Aparārka, who tried to make clear the complications of Manu and Yajña-valkya respectively and put the views of ancient authors in a simple manner. Thus their works are very valuable for the students of mediaeval Hindu polity.

---

1. *Kṛtyakalpa.*, (Introduction) p. 10.
2. *H. D. S.*, vol. III, (Introduction), p. xix.

The *Suvarṇabhāsottama Sūtra*, a Mahāyana Buddhist text, though belonging to a somewhat earlier period, was very influential amongst the Buddhists of India and abroad at this time. Though it is mainly religious in its contents, it is unlike most other Mahāyana texts in that it has sections dealing with the origin and divinity of kingship, and the royal duties and giving advice to kings to be pacifist in their outlook.

Some of the *Purāṇas* were written in our period, amongst which the *Agni Purāṇa* and the Jaina *Mahā Purāṇa* are very important for our purpose. The great value of the *Mahā Purāṇa* is that it contains a considerable amount of Jaina historical tradition, which is hardly available in other sources. The same is the case with the *Matsya Purāṇa.*

The historical literature of India of our period is not abundant, though it is certainly not so meagre as it has been stated by Dr. P.N. Banerjea.[1] Our most important source of this type is the *Rājataraṅgini* of Kalhaṇa, which deals with the kings of Kashmir and throws useful light upon the politics of the period. Next in importance comes the *Prabandhacintāmaṇi*, of the Jaina Merutuṅgācārya. It is written in prose and is a compilation of several stories dealing with the different ruling dynasties of Western India of our period. The Sanskṛt *Hammīra Mahākāvya* and the early Hindi *Pṛthvirājarāso* also throw very useful light upon the chronology of the Caūhān dynasty and the attitude of the rulers towards their subjects.

The writings of Harṣa of Kanauj, Bāṇa, Bhoja, Sandhyākaranandin, Rājaśekhara and others give valuable information about the political condition of India of our period. The famous *Kathāsaritsāgara* of Somadeva contains several stories which are important for the students of politi cal thought of the Hindus.

Some light is also thrown upon the subject by the accounts of the foreign travellers, such as Hiuen-Tsiang, Al-Bīrūnī, Sulaiman the merchant, Al-Masūdi and others, who visited India, and noticed the attitude of the kings towards their subjects, and they are very valuable from our point of view.

The epigraphic records are invaluable. They elucidate certain facts more definitely than do the other sources. The

1. *Public Administration in Ancient India*, p. 6.

inscriptions are dated, which makes it possible to ascribe the matter contained in them to a definite period. They show how some early mediaeval kings owed their origin to their power of sword; others trace their origin from divine ancestors and thus shed light on their superhuman character. Moreover, many inscriptions, mostly land grants, help us to understand the nature of the ownership of land in our period.

In this work we have attempted a thorough study of mediaeval North Indian kingship, both in theory and practice. We have tried to explain concept of kingship and we have also endeavoured to show how the Indian ideas of kingship are comparable with the thought of Plato and Dante on the same subject. We have given considerable space to the ideas on the origin of kingship current in our period. Earlier students have tried to establish the existence of four different doctrines[1] of kingship —divine, social-contract, patriarchical and magical. But by the beginning of our period even the Buddhists had harmonised their doctrine of kingship with the Hindu sources and taught the divine origin of kingship. We have taken into account the view of Dr. Banerjea[2] who maintains a doctrine of the patriarchical origin of kingship; we find that the stories of the *Mahā Purāṇa* rather indicated a belief in the origin of king from a tribal magician.[3] References to the origin of kingship by force have also been considered.

The earlier authors whom we have considered accept the existence of the doctrine of the divinity of kingship with certain limitations and they are hesitant to accept the existence of the doctrine of the king's full divinity in India, but we are going to consider the problem in greater detail and see how Indian[4] deas of king's divinity are comparable with those of other ancient cultures.

Some modern historians of ancient India have stated that monarchy was limited,[5] that kingship was a trust[6] and that the

---

1. *Some Aspects of Ancient Hindu Polity*. p. 127 ff., Ghoshal, p. 376, *Public Administration In Ancient India*, p. 38. *S. G. A. I.*, p. 17.
2. *Public Administration in Ancient India*, p. 38.
3. *Infra*. pp. ff.
4. *Infra.*, pp. 121 ff.
5. *South Indian Polity*, p. 20.
6. *S. G. A. I.*, p. 65.

king's chief function was to please the people.[1] In our study we have tried to consider whether and how far these generalisations are correct for the early mediaeval period.

The ultimate ownership of land is a matter of great controversy, and Indian scholars have almost invariably stated that individual ownership of land existed in India. An examination of their arguments and consideration of evidences from the *Kātyāyana Smṛti*, the *Bṛhaspat Smṛti*, and Medhātithi's commentary along with archaeological sources and foreign accounts form the main part of the topic.

Further, we have considered that though ahead of their time Indian theoreticians advised their king to maintain friendly relations with all and to remain satisfied with what they had. In case of threat, they were advised to join the *maṇḍala* and to live in peace and prosperity. War was regarded as the last resort of Indian diplomacy. Rulers were expected to wage war only when they were strong enough to subdue the enemy. Rulers were advised to care for the interest of vanquished people in their countries.

Thus the present work can claim to be the first study to consider together the different aspects of kingship in the period concerned. We have attempted to study afresh the more important points of controversy and to give our conclusions for whatever they are worth. Though we have presented a less happy picture of Hindu kingship than many great scholars, we have tried to follow the sources where they have led us, and hope that, in doing so, we have contributed something in the knowledge of India's past.

1. *H. A. I.*

CHAPTER II

CONCEPT OF KINGSHIP

On the authority of the verse referring to the various constituents[1] of *rājya* Prof. Bhandarkar[2] held that the concept of state was prevalent in ancient India. He argued that had the word *rājya* been used in the sense of king's dominion there was no need to use the word *janapada* or *rāṣṭra* for territory. The word *janapada* has been interpreted by Dr. Jayaswal[3] for a collective body. Kāmandaka[4] used this word in the sense of people. It is used in the sense of people in the *Mahābhārata*[5] and other texts. In addition to this Prof. Bhandarkar himself has used the word *janapada* for population.[6] Besides this the word *rāsṭra* is used in the sense of people in the *Mahābhārata*.[7] There is reference to the same effect in the *Atharvaveda*[8] where the earth is invoked to impart strength and brilliance to the *rāṣṭra*. Brilliance and strength can be imparted to people only and not to the soil of the nation. Thus it seems that the terms *janapada* and *rāṣṭra* stand for people, and hence *rājya* may be taken to include kingdom.

Prof. Altekar[9] has furthered Prof. Bhandarkar's point by quoting *Rājya*, *Bhaujya*, *Vairājya* and *Svarājya* as various types of states. The quotation from the *Aitareya Brāhmaṇa* cited by Prof. Altekar reads, "The divine Sādhyas and Apatyās inaugurated Indra in the middle region, which is a firmly established footing (the immovable centre) to the kingship (*rājya*). Hence, the king of Kurupañcāla with the Vaśas and Usinaras are inaugurated to the kingship and called kings." The word is again used in the sense of territory ruled by the king and we find *rājā*

1. *Svāmyamātya janapadadurga koṣadaṇḍamitrāṇiprakṛtayaḥ*. *Kaut.* vi. 1, p. 257.
2. *Some Aspects of Hindu Polity*, p. 65.
3. *Hindu Polity*, p. 270, *footnote* 47.
4. *Kāma*. iv. ver. 51-52.
5. M. M. Williams, *A Sanskṛit English Dictionary*, p. 379.
6. *Some Aspects of Hindu Polity*, p. 69.
7. *A Sanskṛt English Dictionary* by M. M. Williams, p. 879.
8. *Atharvaveda*, xii. i. 8 & 10.
9. *State and Government in Ancient India*, p. 20.

being inaugurated in his kingdom. Thus *rājya* stands for kingdom rather than a modern state.

According to Prof. Laski[1] "The state, it is urged, is in fact, the supreme coercive power in a given political society." This coercive power vested in a given political society forms the basis of state. But the study of Lakṣmīdhara,[2] Caṇḍaśvara,[3] Medhātithi,[4] Aparārka[5] and others show that this coercive power was vested in the hands of *rājā*. Secondly, we shall see later that the economy of the territory was controlled by the king and not by the people as it is done in a modern state. Thirdly, the rule of an individual encourages inequality in society. Hence, we find Kāmandaka[6] stating that a monarch should never promote a high-born with a low-born one. Had there been any sense of equality in the mind of the Hindu theoretician he would have never stated such a thing because the modern state does not make any distinction between the rich and the poor, nobody to-day would say that poor people have no right of existence, and the poor at least in law, get the same privileges as the rich people get. Such inequality is possible only in a monarchical form of government. Fourthly, in a modern state the omnipotence of the state is recognised, and the allegiance of the people is demanded in the name of the state. If the state happens to be a constitutional monarchy, people pay their allegiance to the king in the parliament. But all the sources belonging to our period refer to the omnipotence of the king which was recognised, except as theoretically limited by the claims of *dharma*, and the allegiance of the people was demanded for the king only, and not for any other governmental organ. For example we can quote Somadeva,[7] who while prescribing criteria for envoys, stated that they should be *svāmibhakta*. Kāmandaka[8] made a similar statement.

Thus the above discussions would show that ancient Indian political thinkers used the word *rājya* for king's dominion and not the state.

---

1. *Grammer of Politics*, (*Introduction*), p. 2.
2. *Kṛtyakalpataru*, p. 2.
3. *Rājanītiratnākara*, p. 2.
4. *Medhātithi on Manu.*, vii. ver. 5.
5. *yāj.* ver. 311 & 33.
6. *Kām.*, ch. 5, ver. 70.
7. *N. V.*, p. 171.
8. *Kām.*, iv. ver. 25.

The Jaina *Ācārāṅga Sūtra*, in a well known passage, strongly disapproves of any form of government at all similar to democracy in the modern sense. The verse[1] in question states that monks should not visit the country where there is no king, where the crown prince reigns, where there are two kings, where the government is ineffective or where there is republican form of government. The statement makes it clear that *gaṇarājya*, which must have approached more closely than other Indian systems the modern democratic state, was not approved. The rule of the crown prince and division of sovereignty was not liked. Danger to the security of life and property was feared in a kingless state.

Besides these Medhātithi[2] interpreted the term *rājya* in the sense of kingdom. The text reads, "If the king, through folly, harasses his own kingdom, he with his kin soon looses his *rājya* and life." There is a similar reference in Kāmandaka[3] where *rājya* apparently stands for kingdom. It can be deduced from a passage in the *Suvarṇabhāsottama Sūtra*,[4] which reads that the king should give up his life and *rājya* rather than abandon *dharma*, that the word *rājya* refers to the kingdom and nothing else.

Thus we find that almost all authorities of ancient India used the word *rājya* in the sense of king's dominion. Therefore, it seems that it was the king's dominion which was a more popular form of government than any other.

At one place, Kauṭilya[5] suggested that king is the kingdom. A similar attitude seems to have been adopted by the Jaina author Somadeva,[6] who stated that king is in the root of all politics, which points out king's suzerainty over all the *prakṛtis* of the kingdom. Śukra[7] held "that no man other than a king is competent to rule and pacify the earth" which makes us think that persons other than the king were not considered

1. *Āca.*, ii, 3. 10.
2. Medhātithi on Manu, VII. ver. III.
3. Kām., ch. XIII, ver. 81.
4. Tyajecca jīvitaṃ rājyaṃ dharmārthaṃ viṣayasyaca / ch. 12, v. 53 Nobel Edition.
5. *Kauṭilya Arthaśāstra*, VIII, p. 332.
6. *N. V.*, ch. 17, ver. 3, p. 180.
7. *Śukra*, I, ver. 356.

competent to rule. Hence, it appears that people believed in monarchy more than anything else.

Kingship is defined by Aristotle[1] as the rule of one for the common good of the kingom and the supreme power of the kingdom, according to him, is vested in the king. Dante[2] has justified this rule of a single individual in the following words:—

"And it is better, wherever possible, for something to be performed by one single means rather than by several...But mankind is capable of being governed by a single supreme prince who is monarch."

So said the Hindu theoretician Śukra[3] that "there should ever be only one leader in the kingdom, never many." We are not in a position to discuss why Śukra and other authors advocated kingship only, because none of them provide any explanation of it. But such passages show that the location of the supreme power in what would now be termed oligarchy or democracy was not approved of, though its possibility was recognised in this period with the occurrence of the word *gaṇa* in an inscription from Mayurbhanj[4] which has been translated as meaning republic by Dr. R.C. Majumdar, the editor of the text.

It would appear that even at this late period some tribes on the fringes of Hindu culture were still governed by a tribal assembly, or at least by non-hereditary chiefs, and thus an alternative to monarchy was not wholly unknown to our theorists. Śukra[5] probably thought, like Dante, that the rule of many was needless when a single person could run the administration properly. But in another place he stressed[5] importance of the councillors and other officers. Therefore, the rule of one appears to have stood for the rule of the king with the help of the ministers and other assistants.

Let us examine what the Indian political thinkers thought about the institution of kingship. Śukra[6] held that a sovereign is always possessed of the attributes of seven persons, i.e., father,

---

1. *Politics*. Book III, ch. vii, p. 78 (Everyman's Library).
2. *Monarchy*, pp. 22 ff.
3. Sadaikanāyakaṃ rājyaṃ kuryānna bahunāyakam I *Śukra*. 1, 682.
4. *E. I.*, vol. 25, p. 162.
5. *Śukra*, 1, ver. 189-90.
6. *Śukra*. 1, ver. 153-60.

mother, preceptor, brother, friend, Kuvera and Yama. As a father provides his offspring with attributes (i.e. by education) so the king should endow his subjects with good qualities. The mother pardons offences and nourishes the children (so as the king). The *guru* is an advisor to the disciple, and teaches him good lessons (so also the king). The brother takes out his own legal share of the ancestral property (so also the king receives his own share of the people's wealth and property). The friend is the confident and keeper (or protector) of one's self, wife, wealth, and secrets (so also the king). Kuvera gives wealth (so also the king), and Yama is punisher (so also the king). The *Mahā Purāṇa*[1] stated that Nābhirāja advised his people like a father for their well-being. The Buddhist text *Suvarṇabhāsottama Sūtra* put the king in the same category as parents,[2] and stated that the king and parents were both responsible for the performance of good deeds. The *Matsya*[3] *Pūrāṇa* stated "that the king should be like father and brother to his subjects." All these citations from different sources suggest that the relation between the people and the king was considered to be same as between the members of the family. The whole nation was taken as family, and the king as the father or the eldest male member of the family. As in a patriarchial family the eldest member was the head of the family by virtue of his wide experience, so was the king in the case of the nation, as the family head should look after the family business, collect money earned by different members of the family, and take the responsibility of the intellectual, moral and physical welfare of the family members, so was it expected of the king in the case of kingdom as a whole, without making any distinction of caste or creed—a distinction which was deeply rooted in the early Indian society, but which did not, in the minds of the theorists, affect the king's responsibility of protecting and caring for all his subjects.

This paternal concept of kingship appears to have been very strong in Indian minds because from the beginning of our history we find traces of it. One of the separate Kaliṅga[4] edicts of Aśoka records "All men are my children, and just as I desire

1. *M. P.*, ch. 111, ver. 211-212, p. 64.
2. *S. Sūtra.*, ch. 13, p. 126, Nanjio Edition.
3. *Mat.*, ch. 215, ver. 57.
4. Bhandarkar, *Aśoka*, p. 63.

for my children that they obtain every kind of welfare and happiness in this and the next world, so do I desire for all men," which agrees with a statement made in the Kauṭilya Arthāśāstra[1] where the relation between the king and the subjects is said to be that of father and childr en. Thus both in the early and mediaeval period we see that the paternal concept of kingship was approved, and the king was hailed as the father of the nation. This is very near to the idea propounded by Aristotle,[2] "The government of the children should be kingly, for the power of the father over the child is founded in affection and seniority, which is a species of kingly government, for which reason Homer very properly calls Jupiter "the father of Gods and men", who was king of both these, for nature requires that a king should be the same species with those whom he governs, though superior in some particulars, as is the case between the elder and the younger, the father and the son."

According to the Kāmandaka[3] "the king, ministers, kingdom, castle, treasury, army and allies are the seven limbs of the monarchy; good sense and unebbing energy are its primary stay." Aparāka commenting upon Yājñavalkya[4] held that "it is the king's duty to protect the kingdom, there are seven constitutents of monarchy. Thus there are seven limbs." Medhātithi[5] held that the king, minister, kingdom, the people, the treasury, the army, and the ally—these are the seven constituents, and the kingdom is described as having seven limbs." Śukra[6] held that kingship is an organism of seven limbs, namely the sovereign, the minister, the friend, the treasury, the army, the ally, and the people. Of these seven constituents of kingship, the king or the sovereign is the head, the minister is the eye, friend is the ear, treasure is the m outh, the army is the mind, the fort is the arm and the people are the legs. Thus the whole nation was regarded as an organic body of this Indian political thinker. It is worth noting that the idea of the nation as an organic body seems to have grown stronger in process of time,

1. *Tānapitevānugṛhnuyāt* l *Arthaśāstra II*, Quoted by Dikshitar in *H.A.I.*, p. 74.
2. *Politics*, Book I, ch. xii, p. 22.
3. *Kām.*, ch. i, ver. 16.
4. *Aparārka on Yāj*, 1. 351, p. 588.
5. *Medhātithi on Manu.*, ix. 294, vol. v., p. 219.
6. 1, V. 121-24 (B.K. Sirkar's version).

because the earlier authors merely referred to the seven limbs without pressing the analogy, but in Śukra, one of the later authorities, we find a well balanced comparison between the organic body and the nation. A remarkable aspect of this concept of Indian thought in our period is that all different limbs were often regarded as equal. Thus Medhātithi commenting upon the different limbs of the nation held[1]: "Each is dependant upon the others." This very idea is further emphasised : "Since their qualities are mutually helpful to one another, there can be no distinction among them; just as there is none between the soil, the seed and the water in the process of cultivation. From this it follows that proper attention should be given to every one of them." He further commented[2] : "There certainly is some difference in their relative importance, what then is meant by the assertion that no one of them is superior is that due care should always be taken in the guarding of the ally and the other limbs also, which in the preceeding verse have been declared to be of minor importance, because the destruction of the ally also would eventually lead to the destruction of the king's own kingdom, especially when the attack upon the former comes from a powerful quarter, even though the danger may not be imminent. There is nothing that is not helpful to the king; there may be some purpose that is served by inferior agents but not by superior agents. Hence, every one of the constituents should be carefully attended to; that is, the people should not be harassed by unfair punishments and they should always be guarded against robbers and other dangers. Kāmandaka[3] held that "different limbs contributed to one another's weal and the loss of a single one of them renders the whole imperfect, he who wishes to keep administration perfect, should study well their natures." The *Matsya Purāṇa*[4] stated "Each of the seven limbs are complementary to others."

Thus the whole nation was thought of as one organic body, and the different constituents as the different limbs of that body. As the perfection of every limb is essential for the good physique of the body, so the competence of each constituent was regarded

1. *Medhātithi on Manu.*, ix. ver. 296.
2. *Ibid.*, ver. 297.
3. *Kām.*, iv. 1-2.
4. *Matsya*, ch. 220, vol. 9, p. 233.

as necessary for the well being of the nation as a whole. Hence, we find Kāmandaka, Aparārka and others as seen above, declaring that the king should try to keep every constituent perfect by paying proper attention to it, which is comparable to Dante's[1] analogy of the different parts of the whole. He stated :—

"Furthermore, the order of a part stands in the same relation to the order of the whole as the part does to the whole; therefore, the order within a part has as its end the order of the whole, which brings it to perfection. Hence, the goodness of the order amongst the parts does not surpass the goodness of the total order, in fact the reverse is true. Now in all things this twofold order is to be found; that is, the relation of the parts towards each other and the relation of parts to that unity which is not itself a part (in the same way that the parts of an army are related towards each other yet are all subordinated to the commander). Hence, the relation of the parts to that unity is the superior of the two orders; and the other relation is simply a function of the superior order, not vice versa. Now if this pattern of relationship is found in individual groups of human beings it must apply all the more to mankind as a group or whole, in virtue of the previous syllogism concerning the superior pattern of relationship. But it has been adequately proved in the previous chapter that this pattern is in fact found in all human groups, therefore, it should also be found in the whole.

Consequently, all those parts below the level of a kingdom, as well as kingdom themselves, must be subordinate to one ruler or rule, that is to the monarch."

Kāmandaka held that "a sovereign discharging his duty according to the rules of polity soon secures *Trivarga* for himself and his subjects." Similarly Śukra[3] held that "if the king proceeds according to the dictates of *nīti* he can supply himself as well as his subjects with *Trivarga* or virtue, wealth and enjoyment; otherwise he destroys them both." Bṛhaspati[4] stated: "The fruit of *nīti* is the attainment of righteousness, wealth and

1. *Monarchy*, p. 11.
2. Kam., ch. I, ver. 13, ch. II, ver. 77.
3. *Śukra*, I, ver. 133-34.
4. *Bṛhaspāti Arthaśāstra*, ch. 2, ver. 43.

enjoyment." Somadeva paid tribute to the king who yields *dharma*, *artha*, and *kāma*. The Buddhist text *Suvarṇabhāsottama Sūtra* tells us that four great hereditary kings promised the Lord Buddha to look after the spiritual welfare of the people by means of righteousness. It is an universal doctrine of Hinduism that of three aims *dharma* is of greater importance than the other two. Thus the king's primary function was thought of as promoting the religious merit. The two lesser aims were often looked upon as mere means towards the higher one. This topic has been dealt with in greater detail in the *Mārkaṇḍeya Purāṇa*, thus "the king, in whose kingdom, O my child, the duties of various orders and *aśramas* do not suffer deterioration, attains eternal happiness both in this world and in the next. To establish persons in their own religion, which is being disturbed by the wicked people, constitutes the paramount of a king and leads to his success."

From the above quotation we find that Indian theoreticians often looked on kingship embeded in religion which is in consonance with the ideas propounded by Max Müler[1] and Bloomfield.[2]

These statements of Indian authors on the king's duty to promote the *Trivarga* with the aim of enhancing his own and his subjects religious merit, we may compare it with the thought of Plato[3] which runs as follows :—

"We are therefore ready to maintain that, whether it be in the infinity of past time, or in the future, or even at the present in some country beyond our horizons, whenever men skilled in Philosophy take part in politics, then the society we have described either exists or existed or will exist, and the spirit of philosophy herself gain control. No possibility is involved. What we have described is admittedly difficult but it is not impossible."

Śukra[4] stated that the king is the cause of the prosperity of this world, is respected by the experienced and old people and gives pleasure to the eyes (of the people) as the moon to the sea. If the king is not a perfect guide, his subjects will get

1. *History of Sanskṛt Literature*, 1859, p. 31.
2. *Religion of the Vedas*. pp. 4-5.
3. *The Republic*, pp. 261-262.
4. *Śukra*, 1, ver. 127-32.

into trouble, as a boat without a helmsman sinks in a sea. Without the governor, the subjects do not keep to their own spheres. Nor does the sovereign flourish in the world without subjects. In the later portion of this work Śukra[1] further stated : "The king is the maker of the age and the promulgator of duties and sins. The faults are to be ascribed neither to the age nor to the subjects but to the king. Men practise that by which the king is satisfied. Why should they follow his teachings through greed or fear ? Where the king is virtuous, people are also virtuous, where the king is a sinner, subjects are also vicious." The passage in question shows that the king was expected to act as a leader of the people. It was he who established the current standards of right and wrong. If he gave a successful lead, prosperity was presumed to prevail, otherwise the destruction of the people was to be expected. So the king was held responsible for the activity of the people. Kāmandaka laid much emphasis upon this point. He stated[2]: "The king is the cause of the prosperity and progress of the world and is held in high estimation even by the grown-up people, he affords delight to the eye of men, even as the moon affords delight unto the (mighty) ocean. If a ruler of men does not lead his subjects on the path of rectitude, then are these latter (hopelessly) tossed about in the rough sea." This suggested that the prestige of the king was subject to the capacity of lordship, if he gave a firm and righteous lead the prosperity of the people was expected to follow and if he did not, the people would be in desparate trouble.

Kāmandaka[3] made it clear how a king was to give such moral leadership to his people. "In the first instance, a king should direct his ministers; and the dependants and then his subjects to do the same. A self controlled king whose subjects are devoted to him and who is careful in protecting his subjects earns great prosperity for himsef." He further stated: "How can one, who is not capable enough of subjugating his own mind, hope to subjugate this (extensive) earth bounded with oceans themselves ?" Here we see that stress is laid upon the king serving as a model to his subjects. It is only by control-

---

1. *Śukra*, iv. sec. 1, ver. 116-121.
Kāma., ch. 1, ver. 9-10.
Kāma., ch. 1, ver. 23-24.

ling his senses that he can set an example to his people in order that they may control their own sense. Thus the quotations from Śukra, Kāmandaka and others suggest that self-control on the part of the king will be followed by self-control on the part of the people, which would lead them to prosperity and virtue This again is similar to Plato's discourse[1] "It was for these reasons and with all this in mind, I said that we felt bound in all honesty, though with some trepidation, to say that there would never be a perfect state or society or individual until some chance compelled this minority of uncorrupted philosophers, now called useless, to take a hand in politics, willy-nilly, and compelled society to listen to them; or else until providence inspired some of our present rulers and kings or their sons, with a genuine love of true philosophy."

Śukra[2] held that "the strong is always the enemy of weak." B.K. Sarkar attempted to expand this passage in the following words. "Of course, if there is a struggle for existence the fitter and more powerful can be known only by their survival. In all ages and among all people it has been found that in day to day life, the stronger tends to put obstacles in the road to the prosperity of the weaker. It can be gathered from many statements that in our period the infringement of the property right of the poor by the rich was always feared. Therefore, it is stated : that a king[3] is created for the preservation of living creatures. Medhātithi[4] commenting upon Manu, has made the point more specific. He held "If punishment was not inflicted, then the stronger, i.e., those possessed of greater power, or more energetic or wielding weapons, or being larger in numbers, would have roasted the weaker, like fish, on the spit, i.e., just as fish is roasted on a spit for wood, so would the less powerful be treated by the more powerful, by suffering more pecuniarily as well as physically, and also by being deprived of their wives and so forth. For this reason the king should untiringly punish those that deserve punishment, and he should not entertain any such notions as "How can I carry on investigation into the matter ? I shall not punish anyone at all."

1. *The Republic*, Book VI, part VII, p. 261.
2. *Śukra*, I, ver. 99 (B.K. Sarkar's version).
3. *Matsya*, ch. 226, ver. 1.
4. *Medhātithi on Manu.*, vii, 21.

Hence, we find that the well-being of the whole people was expected to flow from the leadership and good government of the king. This can again be compared with Plato's philosopher ruler. "He will, I suppose, as he works look frequently at his model, the ideals of justice and beauty and discipline and similar qualities, and again at the copy of them he is trying to make in human nature, mixing and blending trials to give the colour of manhood, and taking always as his pattern that quality in men that Homer called godly and godlike. He will sometimes delete and draw again, of course, but will go on till he has made human nature as acceptable to God as may be."

Kāmandaka[2] stated: "this world by nature is enslaved to the pleasure of the senses and is ardently longing to enjoy wealth and women. Only when agitated by the fear of punishments a person keeps to the eternal ways of rectitude followed by the pious. Upright conduct is scarce, men only attend to their prescribed duties through fear of punishment even as a respectable woman serves her lean or poor or deformed or diseased husband through fear of the sanction specified in the code of morality. Thus like rivers that flow through right courses, falling into sea, all possibility devolves upon and never dwindles away from a king who, knowing the good and evil of the infliction of punishment, and following the path chalked out by the *Vedas*, framed rules of conduct for his subjects." The same author[3] further stated : "A king by the right infliction of punishments upholds the stayless world that is being forcibly drowned in the lake of sin by lust and cupidity and other such passions." These two passages from Kāmandaka tell us that the king's rod of justice, makes the people perform their respective duties and in its absence there will be confusion in the world. Medhātithi[4] tried to explain why this highest authorities of justice was vested in the king. He stated that "It is only the king who is truthful of speech, who acts after due consideration, who knows the essence of virtue, pleasure and wealth." Thus it was essential to be impartial, considerate and wealthy to administer the kingdom. It was probably

---

1. *Republic*, Book vi, part vii, p. 262.
2. *Kām.*, ch 11, ver. 42-43.
3. *Ibid.*, ver. 41.
4. *Medhātithi on Manu*, vii, ver. 26.

thought by Medhātithi and other Indian thinkers of the age that ordinary people, not possessing those qualities to any high degree, could not carry out the general activities of the government ably; and those qualities were expected to be found in the king, presumably on account of the divinity inherent in him. Therefore, Kāmandaka and other authors look only on the king as the best person to control the people for their own well-being. This is again comparable to Dante's[1] doctrine.

"From which it can be seen that the person wishing to bring the best out of others must himself be in the best condition. But the one in best condition for governing is none other than the monarch.........Therefore, what was said in the minor premises was right, that monarch alone is completely equipped to rule, therefore, the monarch alone is able to bring the best out of others."

Like Dante[2] the Indian philosophers thought the king absolutely necessary for the maintenance of law and justice in the kingdom, but as we have discussed this question at greater length in another chapter[3] there is no need to deal with it further here. As well as exercising judicial authority in his kingdom, it appears that the king also tried to settle the disputes arising amongst his feudal lords. Though none of the theoreticians belonging to our period refers to this particular function of the king yet it can be gathered from different literary sources that the paramount authority interfered in the quarrel of the chiefs of his kingdom. For instance we find that Pratāp Siṃha,[4] one of the chiefs at the court of Pṛthvirāja, could not tolerate the growing prestige of Kaṇha, another feudal lord in the same court. So Pratāp Siṃha attempted to pull out the moustache of Kaṇha in order to humiliate him. Kaṇha only saved his prestige by killing Pratāp Siṃha. Then Ari Siṃha, the younger brother of Pratāp Siṃha, attempted revenge, but he in term was killed by Kaṇha, and the feud continued till Pṛthvirāja himself interfered. There is another reference to this effect in the *Rājatarangiṇī*.[5] A struggle broke out between Sam-

1. *Monarchy*, pp. 20 ff.
2. *Monarchy*, p. 15.
3. Supra.
4. *Pṛthvirājarāso*, pp. 280 ff.
5. *Rāj.*, vii, ver. 533 onwards.

grāmapāla, the son and successor of Sahajapāla of Rājapurī and Madanpāla, the diseased king's brother. Consequently king Kalaśa, as the overlord had to interfere in the matter. Thus the preservation of peace and order among the feudal lords of the kingdom also needed one paramount power who could settle their differences. Therefore, the presence of the king as the paramount power was regarded as essential. For this again we can find a parallel in the work of Dante.[1]

"It is clear that a dispute may arise between two princes, neither of whom is subject to the other, and that this may be their fault or their subjects. Therefore a judgement between them is indispensable. However, since, neither can take cognizance over the other (neither being subject to the other and equals do not rule over equal) there needs to be a third person enjoying wider jurisdiction, who by right rules over both of them. This person must be either monarch......Therefore, monarchy is necessary to the world. And the philosopher appreciated this truth when he wrote : 'things recent being badly ordered, but to have different ruler is bad, therefore, one Prince'."

Thus it appears that the failure of the tribal republic long before our period—inspired people to think of the monarchical form of government as the only guarantee of the peace and prosperity of the people. The seeds of the monarchical form of government were certainly sown in a much earlier period but it is only when we come to this period that we find the ideas of monarchy developed in a mature form which can be compared with the concept of kingship in other mediaeval civilisations.

1. *Monarchy*, p. 14.

Chapter III

ORIGIN AND DIVINITY OF KINGSHIP

Modern historians have expounded different theories on the origin of kingship, social[1] contract, divine,[2] patriarchial,[3] magical, and also theory of Force for early India. Coming to the period under review there is epigraphic evidence to suggest that Gopāla[4] of Pāla dynasty assumed the office of kingship on people's request. There is reference to the same effect in the *Subodhikā*[5] commentary of Vinayavijayagaṇi upon Hemacandṛācārya's *Trishashṭiśalākāpurusha-carita.* It is reported that the twins started to quarrel with one another in the time of Vimalavāhana, and thus *daṇḍanīti* took the form of *hākāra* for light offence. In the time of later *Kulakaras* crimes became severe. The twins approached Lord Nābhi, who advised them to have a king. Hence, they decided accordingly and selected Lord Rishabha as their king who was consecrated by Lord Indra. These are the only two stray examples which refer to the contractual origin of kingship. The Jaina story presents a somewhat complicated problem. It refers to the creation of king by election, but this election was caused at the instance of the *Kulakara.* It is stated in the *Mahā Purāṇa* and other texts that Pratiśruti and other succeeding *Kulakaras* established all kinds of institutions in India. We propose to consider the character of those *Kulakaras* later in this chapter. Meanwhile we would suggest that the story in question only refers to the completion of work once started by *Pratiśruti.* The legend associated with Gopāla may have been the survival of earlier ideas handed down through the Buddhist traditions. Thus the contractual origin of kingship as proposed by Panikkar does not hold any good in our period.

---

1. *A.H.P.*, pp. 127 ff. Origin and Evolution of Kingship in India, pp. 49 ff.
2. *History of Hindu Political Theories*, p. 276.
3. *S.G.A.I.*, p. 17, *State in Ancient India*, p. 372.
4. *E. I.*, vol. iv, p. 249, ver. iv.
5. Quoted in *A History of Indian Political Ideas*, p. 461.

On the other hand we find that the Buddhists along with Hindu authors strengthened the idea of the divine origin of kingship. Both Caṇḍeśvara.[1] and Lakṣmīdhara stated that there was *arājakatā* in the beginning and that the people were dispersed into different directions through fear. So God created the king. The use of the term *arājakatā* is somewhat interesting. The word *arājakatā* has been taken by Panikkar[2] for a period when

"The strong will abduct the wives of the weak
There will be no feeling of this is mine
The rules of morality will not be followed.
The wicked will take away by force (other's) carriage, clothes, ornaments, etc.
People will kill their own parents, old men, teachers, guests, and *gurus*.
Good men will be oppressed and the wicked will be strong.
The rich will live in fear of life and of being imprisoned.
Friendship will not be recognised.
There will be no ploughing, no agriculture and no trade."

Prof. Sharma[3] holds similar view. It refers to a condition of affairs when the just suffers at the hands of the unjust. Conditions obtaining at the start of Indian monarchy are similar to that described by Plato,[4] who states that "when both just and unjust men are wronged, they need the pressure of some supreme authority who may keep them under control." Here we must remember that Plato was talking about the basis of a city state, but the Hindus were talking about the origin of the king. The *Matsya Purāṇa*[5] states, "A king is created by Brahmā for the preservation of all beings, for awarding the *Devas* their respective share of sacrificial oblations, and for inflicting proper punishment on the guilty. King Vikramāditya in the *Praban-*

1. *Arājaka hi Lokesmin Sarvato vidrute bhayāt.* 1
Rakṣārtham asya sarvasya rājānām asṛjāt prabhuḥ 11
p. 2, Kṛtyakalpa, p. 2.
2. *Origin and Evolution of Kingship in India*, p. 32.
3. *Aspects of Political Ideas and Institutions in Ancient India*, p. 39.
4. *Republic*, II, p. 155 (L.C.S.)
5. *Mat.*, 226, 1.

dhacintāmaṇi[1] appeared for the rescue of the people who were terrified of their demon king." All these references suggest that the basic thought behind them is that when in the distant past the unjust dominated the just, the just recognised the necessity of putting a stop to this unhappy situation. So people created city state in Greece, while in Indian tradition they called on God to help them and the latter created the king or the preservation of his creation.

A question may be raised as to the nature of the divinely appointed king. Was he the incarnation of the high God or some ordinary being raised to kingship by divine favour ? The *Matsya Purāṇa*,[2] as quoted above, refers to the special incarnation of a God as the king. Caṇḍeśvara[3] and Lakṣmīdhara also believed in the creation of the king by God, rather than the incarnation of a God as king. Kalhaṇa[4] stated that Prajāpati Kaśyapa caused the Gods, let by Druhina, Upendra and Rudra to descend on the earth and to be first ruler of Kashmir. The *Liṅga*[5] *Purāṇa* states that to remove all kinds of trouble amongst the people God was incarnated in the *Tretā-Yuga*. Hiuen-Tsiang[6] stated "At the beginning of this *Kalpa* he relates when men were homeless savages, a Goddess came down from heaven and after bathing in the Ganges became pregnant. She had four sons, who devided the world among them and built cities and first city built was Champa." Thus we see that both the ideas that (1) God appeared in person as the first king of this universe and (2) that the king was specially created by the high God were prevalent in our period.

Those authors who believed in the special creation professed that this human God was composed of the particles of different Gods. Both Caṇḍesvara and Lakṣmidhara agreeing with Manu, state that, having taken the particles of Indra, the wind, Yama, the sun, fire, Varuna, the moon and Kuvera, God created the king. The idea of the extraction of various particles of the different Gods and their combination in a single person

1. *P.C.*, pp. 2 ff.
2. *Mat.*, ch. 226, v. 1.
3. *R.N.*, p. 2 *Kṛtyakalpa*, p. 2.
4. *Raj.*, 1, v. 26-27.
5. *Linga Purāṇa*, ch. 39, ver. 35-43, p. 61
6. *On Yuan Chwang's Travel in India* by T. Walter, vol. 2, ch. 14, p. 181.

indicates the immense importance of the king's office, as we shall see later.

The devine origin of kingship, as believed in by the Hindus, appears to have influenced the thought of the later Buddhists. During the early days they believed in the Social-contract theory, but coming to this period the only Buddhist source known to us containing passages of political significance, the *Suvarṇa-bhāsottama Sūtra*,[1] contains the idea of the divine origin of the kingship in a somewhat modified form. According to this source, the gods order a certain appointed being to enter into the mother's womb and become a human king, and it is by the order of the gods that this being gets an embryo and is born in the form of a man. The being who is destined to rule as king is appointed by the gods from his conception. Here we have in another form the Hindu concept of the divine origin of kingship which we have considered earlier that the king was born by the order of the Great God.

Dr. Panikkar[2] has denied the magical origin of kingship in India. Dr. Beni Prasad[3] thought that the story in the Jaina text *Mahā Purāṇa* implies a belief in the patriarchical origin of kingship, but it appears that he has either drawn too hasty a conclusion or failed to examine the text thoroughly. Undoubtedly the word *Kulakara* has been used for the first king, Vṛṣabhadeva but the use of the word does not necessarily imply that Vṛṣabhadeva was a patriarch. As far as the text is concerned, Vṛṣabhadeva appears in three different functions as magician, because, sun, moon, Rudra and other smaller divinities were under his control; patriarch because he took pleasure in the happiness of his people like a father, and finally, being the best well-wisher of the people he became the king.[4] Prior to Vṛṣabhadeva there were several *Kulakaras*, who are said to have ruled before him. In order to find out what the function of these *Kulakaras* was thought to be and how they are said to have been regarded by the people, we will give a short summary of the story presented

---

1. S. *Śūtra*, p. 73, ch. vi, Nobel Edition.
2. *Origin and Evolution of Kingship in India*, p. 43.
3. *State in Ancient India*, p. 392.
4. *Sa srīmāniti nityābhoganirataḥ putraiśea pantrairnijaiḥ* l
   Ārūdhapranayairūpā hitadhṛtiḥ siṃhāsanādhyāsitaḥ l
   Ṣakrārkkendupurassaraiḥ suravarairvyūḍh Uasacchāsanaḥ
   Śāsti smāpratiśāsano bhuvamimāmāsindhusīmām Jincḥ ll

in the text.[1] The text begins by stating that the first part of the *Avasarpinī* era called *Suṣamā* lasted four crores of years. People during this part of the era were extremely happy. They had neither mental nor physical worries. They were powerful and influential. Women were devoted to their husbands. They took food equal to a *badarī* fruit in measurement daily and lived a very long life. This period corresponds to the golden age (*Kṛtayuga*) of the other sources. With the passage of time came the second phase of the *Suṣamā* period, the light of the *Kalpavṛkṣas,* which illumined the world and provided for the needs of the people, and the bodily strength and the longevity of men began to decline, and this continued until the third phase of the *Suṣamā*. By the close of its third phase the light of the *Kalpavṛkṣas* became extremely dim. Afterwards, on a morning of a full moon day of the month Āṣāḍha, the setting sun and the rising moon appeared. At their appearance the people were very surprised and disturbed. By this time the first *Kulakara* called Pratiśruti had appeared. He was handsome and brighter than the sun because of his sublime radiance. In addition to this he was acquainted with the previous deeds of the people by virtue of his magical power. So he was regarded as the wisest among mankind. He used to observe the phenomena of nature, which was becoming more and more obvious as the *kalpavṛkṣas* grew dim, and explain them to the frightened people. Many of his speeches were very pleasing and consoling to them. When the sun and moon appeared he said to the frightened people, "these two unfamiliar things are called sun and moon, they are the personification of the great light and they always rotate round the sky. Till recently their strength was overshadowed by the light of the *kalpavṛkṣas,* but with the progress of the time the light of the *kalpavṛkṣas* has declined. Therefore they are visible. They are harmless, so you should not be afraid of them." Having heard this people were relieved of their worries, and dispersed after paying him great respect. Afterwards Pratiśruti, and other succeeding *kulakaras,* established all kinds of institutions in India. This in short is the Jaina story of the origin of kingship. This story does neither refer to the joint

1. *M. Purāṇa,* III, 43-70. pp. 49 ff.

family nor Pratiśruti as the head of the family which forms the basis of patriarchical origin of kingship. On the other hand it refers to Pratiśruti as different person than those gathering around him. We are told in this story that Pratiśruti was a great man, who knew all the secrecy of the nature and previous birth of the people. He was well versed in making speeches, which are said to have been delivered through his glittering teeth, and he consoled and contented his people in their bad days. These characteristics of Pratiśruti remind us of the medicine man as described by Sir James Frazer,[1] who tells of the activities of the *Orkoiyot* (or the principal medicine man) among the Nandi of East Africa. According to Frazer the *Orkoiyot* is a diviner and foretells the future by casting stones, inspecting entrails, interpreting dreams, and prophesying when he is drunk. The Nandi believe implicitly in his powers. He tells them when to begin planting their crops; in times of drought he procures rain for them either personally or with the help of other rain makers who are well versed in this craft; he makes woman and cattle fruitful, and no war party can expect to be successful if he has not approved of the foray. His office is hereditary and his person is regarded as absolutely saved. No body may approach him with weapons in his hand or speak in his presence unless the great man addresses him; and it is most important that no body should touch his head else it is feared that his power of divination and so forth would depart from him. However, one of these pontiffs was clubbed to death, being held responsible for several public calamities, to wit, famine, sickness and defeat in war. Thus, like the medicine man of East Africa, Pratiśruti appears to be thought of as a diviner. Certainly nothing is said about his making the cattle and women of his locality fruitful, or about his blessing fighting parties, which is probably because the Jaina tradition does not believe that war existed in the primitive period. But this observance of nature, his interpretation of the past, his outshining the sun by means of his rediance and his holding the teeth give him a magical character.

During the life time of the second *Kulakara*, Sanmati, tiger and other fierce animals made their appearance. People were

1. *Golden Bough*, col. 1, p. 344.

frightened of them and they assembled round the *Kulakara*. Sanmati by means of his magical power removed their fear. People were very grateful for this act of Sanmati, and wished him to be their king.[1]

The magical character of the *Kulakra* is further emphasised in the description of Cakṣusman. It is said that at first parents used to die painlessly soon after the birth of their children, who were invariably twins, but in Cakṣusman's time they began to survive for some time, which was again (strangely enough) frightening for them. So they gathered round the *Kulakara*, who removed their fear by uttering a charm.

According to the Jaina story, the earlier *Kulakaras* appear chiefly in the capacity of medicine man but the later ones take on more of the character of kings, like the magician-kings of the East African Nandi. As the world declined their leadership was at first completely natural, and based solely on popular acceptance, on account of their superior power and wisdom; later it became more formalized and less spontaneous. Thus it is stated that Vṛṣabhadeva, the fourteenth *Kulakara*, had to make promises to maintain the economic solidarity and good administration of the people[2] before his predecessor Nābhirāja, and it was only after these promises that he was made king. Thus the contractual origin of kingship does not hold any good in the Jaina text. This in short is the Jaina doctrine of the origin of kingship. The same story is repeated in another Jaina text, the *Harivaṁśa Purāṇa* and *Trishashṭisalākāpurusha-carita.*

The magical character of the king is further strengthened by the writing of the Buddhist king Harsavardhana.[3] Priyadarśikā, the main actress of his drama, had lost her sense. The king reciting incantations, put his hands over her and she was found gaining sense. Her cousin Vāsavadatta, paid his reverence to the king for this act and his chamberlain appreciated the king's mastery over the act of magic.

Thus it appears from the foregoing discussions that magicians may have won the confidence of people's benefit and

---

1. *Ayam sanmatirevāstu prabhurnaḥ sanmatipradaḥ* |
Iti praśasya saṃpūjya yayuste taṃ svamāspadam ||

M. Purāṇa, III, 89, p. 53.

2. *H.P.*, ch. 7, ver. 125-178 & ch. 9, ver. 43-45.
3. *Priyadarśikā Act.* iv, p. 88.

people on their part may have accepted the magician as their king.

Besides these, origin of kingship by force was not a lost subject. There is a reference to this effect in Merutuṅgācārya[1] where an ordinary person has been found assuming the office of kingship by killing a demon who had harassed people like anything. It has been stated in the *Pṛthvirājarāso*[2] that Kalhaṇa became the king of Kalhaṇapur by his own powers and in the dynasty of Kalhaṇa after a several generations king Anaṇgapāla was born. Hiuen Tsiang[3] recorded: "The king's name is Bhāskaravarman, his title is Kumāra. From the time that this family seized the land and assumed the government till the present king, there have elapsed a thousand succession." Occurrence of 'this family seized the land' refers to the forceful origin of the institution of kingship in Assam.

Thus we see that the theories of divine, magical and origin of kingship by force were known to the theorists of the period under consideration.

Dr. Panikkar[4] refutes the statement of Manu in the following words "that even an infant king should not be despised is only an emphasis on the majesty of the kingship not on the divinity of his person." On the other hand there is an interesting reference to the divinity of the king in the *Suvarṇabhāsottam*[5] *Sūtra*. It is asked "How does a king, who is born of man be called devine ? Why is a king called the son of the Gods ? In reply to this it is said: "By the authority of the great Gods he enters his mother's womb. First he is ordained by the gods only then he finds embryo. What though he is born or dies in the world of mortals arising from the Gods he is called the son of the Gods." Thus what to speak of Hindus, we find even, Buddhists accepting the divinity in the period under review.

Divinity of kingship has been regarded conditional by the modern historians[6] of ancient India. Prof. Bhandarkar referred to passages which do not cover our period. Prof.

1. *P.C.*, p. 23.
2. *P.R.* pp. 258-9, verse. 17.
3. *Buddhist Record of the Western World*, vol. II, Book II, p. 196.
4. *Origin and Evolution of Kingdom in India*, p. 41.
5. *S. Sūtra*, ch. vi. p. 73, Nobel Edition.
6. *A.H.P.*, p. 159 ff., *S.G.A.I.*, p. 62.

Altekar and Panikkar quoted Śukra[1] and stated that an unrighteous king was regarded demon. But the passage in question was intended to prove the superiority of the righteous king over the unrighteous. Besides this, the comparison of an unrighteous king to a demon king is a figure of speech and not a practical formula. So we cannot rely upon such evidences as showing that the king's divinity had any constitutional qualifications.

On the other hand there are a number of examples which suggest that the full divinity of the institution of kingship was widely propounded and accepted in the India of our period. But before we proceed to consider the subject it will be useful to inquire into the reasons that may have led the king and his court to give serious thought.

We have already seen that the first reason may have been the divine origin of kingship propounded by different Indian texts. From this it was but a short step to the view that, as the first king had been divine, so were his successors.

Another important reason leading to the idea of the king's divinity may have been the concept of the king as the begetter of the prosperity of the people. For example, Lakṣmīdhara stated[2] that the king is like Indra because he showers prosperity upon the people—an idea which is similar to that of Homer, who stated that "it was the king who caused the black earth to bring forth wheat and barley, the trees to be loaded with fruits, the flocks to multiply and the sea to yield fish, therefore he is God."[3] In both cases we find the king being accepted as the supernatural being because he was believed to bring prosperity upon the earth.

The next important reason leading to the king's divinity may have been his religious leadership. The *Mārkaṇḍeya Purāṇa*[4] stated that a king who protects the four *varṇas* and four *āśramas* successfully is equal to Śukra (Indra). The *Matsya Purāṇa*[5] stated that by performing religious duties and offering

---

1. *Śukra* I, 139-40, p. 62.
2. *Vārṣikānścaturo'māsān yathendro'bhipravarṣati* |
Tathā bhivarṣethadrāṣṭraṁ kāṁairindravratam caran || ...
Kṛtyakalpa, p. 3.
3. *Quoted by* Hocart in *Kingship*, p. 9.
4. *Mark.*, ch. 27, ver. 31.
5. *Matsya.*, ch. 226, ver. 1.

oblations he satisfies the gods. So he must have been regarded as superior to ordinary beings in the sphere of religious worship. Sandhyākaranandin stated about the Pāla rulers that they checked the unrighteous, encouraged qualified persons, and by performing different kinds of sacrifices supported human being. Thus the satisfaction of the gods by the king's performances of sacrifices may have established his spiritual superiority over his subjects and they may have led his subjects to accept his divinity.

Finally, the absolute character of the kingship would have been another important factor leading to the growth of ideas of the king's divinity. The absolute character of Indian kingship has been denied by the modern historians of ancient India and it is beyond the scope of this chapter to enter into the controversy; we propose to enquire about the character of kingship in a later chapter and to see whether Indian kingship was absolute. Therefore, we shall provisionally conclude this topic with one or two citations from the original authorities, Śukra declared that "Sometime[1] a king, though well qualified, may be without subjects or rights but the subjects, however, vicious, must not be without a king. Just as Indrāni is never a widow, so also the subjects." Nārada[2] states that "As a husband though feeble must be constantly worshipped by his wife, in the same way a ruler though worthless must be constantly worshipped." Hence, we see that presence of absolute king was regarded essential by the same author who stated elsewhere that an unrighteous king is a demon. Even a wicked king was to be respected by the people and constantly worshipped. Had these authors any kind of check on absolute monarchy in their mind, they would have said something else than comparing a wicked ruler with a husband. Thus we see that the question of the limited monarchy in Hindu India does not arise.

These are a few possible factors that may have led kings to boast for their divinity.

---

1. *Prajādhikārahīnassyāt Saguno'pi uṛpaḥ kvacit* l
Na tu nṛpavihīnāssyurdurguṇā hyapi tu prajāh l
Yathā na vidhavendrāṇī sarvadā tu tathā prajāh l
Śukra I, ver. 186-8.

2. *Nirgun'opi yathā strīṇāṃ pujya eva patih sadā* l
Prajanām nirguṇo' pyevaṃ pūjya eva narādhipaḥ ll
Nārada, xviii, v. 22.

Now let us proceed to examine what the Indian authors thought about the divinity of their kings. Lakṣmīdhara,[1] agreeing with Nārada, held that the king endowed with immense power appears in five different forms—Agni, Indra, Soma, Yama and Kuvera. When a king is either justly or without (sufficient) reason, ardent in wrath and burns (or torments) his subjects, he is called Agni. When, relying on his regal power, the king attacks his foe, desirous of victory and upraising a weapon, he is termed Indra. When free from ardent wrath he appears before his subjects with a cheerful countenance, he is said to be Soma. When the king, having seated himself, full of majesty, on the throne of judgement, deals out punishment suitable towards all creatures, he is called Cairasvata (i.e. Yama). When a ruler gladdens with gifts, petitioners, persons commending respect, wisemen, servants and others he is called the God of Riches. Similarly the *Matsya Purāṇa*[2] held that "A king is like the sun because nobody can dare to look at him with hostile eyes, like the moon because he gives satisfaction to all beings by appearing to them, like Yama because he bestows his affection and punishment upon the people according to circumstances, like Varuṇa because he throws his fetters round the feet of the wicked. He curbs the sinners, therefore, he is like Agni, and because the king nourishes all his subjects therefore he is like Pṛthvī." Lakṣmīdhara[3] further stated : "Let the king emmulate the energetic actions of Indra of the sun, of the wind, of Yama, of the moon, of the fire, and of the earth. As Indra sends copious rains during the four months of the rainy season, even so let the king, taking upon himself the office of Indra, shower benefits on his kingdom. As the sun during the eight months (imperceptibly) draws up the water with his rays, even so let him gradually draw his taxes from his kingdom; for that is the office in which he resembles the wind. As Yama at the appointed time subjects to his rule both friends and foes, even so all subjects must be controlled by the king, that is the office in which he resembles Yama. As a sinner is seen bound with ropes by Varuṇa, even so let him

1. *Kṛtyakapla*, pp. 2-3.
2. *Mat.*, *Purāṇa*, 226, ver. 2-8.
3. *Kṛtyakalpa*, pp. 3-4.

punish the wicked, that is the office in which he resembles Varuṇa. He is a king, taking upon himself the office of the moon, whose (appearance) his subjects (great with a great joy) as men feel on seeing the full moon. If he is ardent in wrath against criminals, is endowed with brilliant energy and destroys wicked vassals, then his character is said to (resemble) that of fire. As the earth carries the burden of all beings, so the king takes upon himself the office of the whole earth." Caṇḍeśvara[1] held the same view. Thus we see that each and every movement of the king is compared with that of gods. Moreover, we have seen earlier that the first king was supposed to be composed of the different particles of the different gods. Hence, it can be assumed that theoreticians accepted the divinity of the king and expected that the kings, like the gods, would shower benefits upon the people and yet at the same time punish their enemies and evil doers.

Besides this Lakṣmīdhara,[2] agreeing with Manu,[3] advocated that the king should emulate the energetic actions of Indra, Wind, Yama, Varuṇa, the Moon, Agni and the Earth. The author has used the word *caret* in this connection which gives somewhat a different idea. The term *caret* is in the optative mood and implies that even though the king is not Indra and other divine beings he should try to become so, which lays emphasis on the king's potential divinity.

Furthermore, when considering the character of kingship Lakṣmīdhara,[3] quoting the authority of Manu, held that the king, having considered the matter in hand, his power, and the place, should take on different shapes for the attainment of justice. Therefore, let nobody transgress the royal command. The man, who out of exceeding folly disobeys the king, will undoubtedly perish. For the king quickly makes up his mind to destroy such a man. The natural fire burns only those who are near it, but the king's anger destroys not only that man who disobeys him but the whole of his family together with his cattle and other property. Therefore, even an infant king

1. R.N., p. 4.
2. *Indrasyārkasya vātasya yamasya varuṇsaya ca* l
Somasyā, 'gneḥ pṛthivyāśca tejovṛtaṃ nṛpaścaret ll
Kṛtyakalpa, p. 3.
3. *Kṛtyakalpa*, p. 6.

should not be disobeyed with the thought that he is merely human because a great god resides in him.[1] Lakṣmīdhara here echoes the statement of Manu which shows that the full divinity of kingship was recognised by the Hindu authors of the period. They thought that in the pleasure and anger of the king reside the prosperity and destruction of the people respectively. Therefore, they approved the king's demand for passive obedience.

There is an interesting reference to this effect in the *Suvarṇabhāsottama Sūtra*[2] where it is stated "what though he is born or dies in the world of mortals, arising from the gods he is called the son of gods. The thirty-three great gods assign the fortune of the king. The ruler of the man is created as son of all gods." Thus according to this text it is clear that the king arises from gods and he has been assigned the office of kingship by the gods. Therefore, he is divine and should be respected.

Now let us proceed to consider what the Indian kings themselves thought about their divinity. Talking about ancient Germany A.W. Hocart[3] states that "the ancient German kings and princes traced their lineage back to the individual gods." Like German kings we see that there were many rulers of our period who traced their lineage from different Hindu gods. The Candela king Yaśovarmadeva[4] in an inscription of the 10th century. A.D. traced the family origin from the God Viṣṇu. The Gwalior *praśasti* of the Pratihāra king Bhoja,[5] belonging to the 9th century A.D. recorded the lineage of the Pratihāra dynasty from Lakṣmana, the younger brother of Rāma, who is still believed to be an incarnation of the God Viṣṇu. The Rāṣṭrakūtās of Mankad[6] derived their lineage from the Yadu dynasty, in which Lord Kṛṣṇa is supposed to have born. Sandhyākaranandi[7] tried to establish the relationship between Rāmapala and Rāma the legendary divine Ikṣvāku king. Candravardai[8] thought that

1. *Kṛtyakalpa*, p. 6
2. *S. Sūtra.*, ch. VII.
3. *Kingship*. ch. II.
4. *E.I.*, vol. 1, pp. 129-30.
5. *E.I.*, vol. 18, p. 110, v. 2-4.
6. *E.I.*, vol. 7, p. 215.
7. *R.C.*, pp. 2 ff.
8. *R.P.*, p. 51.

the Cāhamānas were the favourite Kṣatriyas of the Lord Brahmā and derived their origin from the fire God Agni.

The many families of rulers claiming descent from the sun and the moon are too numerous to mention. In general we see that many ruling dynasties of India of our period tried to trace their origin from the well-known Hindu Gods such as Viṣṇu, Rāma, Agni and others; and by establishing their relationship with those Gods they proved themselves divine.

These rulers were not merely satisfied with establishing their descent from Hindu deities, but many of them also considered themselves as incarnations of the Gods—an inference that can be drawn from the *Virudas* such as *Parameśvara*[1] borne by many rulers of our period. The use of the word *parameśvara* suggests that the *Mahārājas* of the period claimed divinity and thought of being Gods.

Now let us examine what the people thought about the divinity of the kings.

From the study of the contemporary literature it appears that it was not only the theoreticians who propounded the doctrine of the divinity of the king, but the people themselves accepted the idea. Sandhyākaranandin[2] talking about the Pāla kings wrote: "Rāma Pāla whom the creator created as a single object combining within himself the spirit of the Lokapālās, Indra, Varuṇa, the wind God, Kuvera and the Sun-God." The poet further held that "He was a veritable incarnation of Hari because his fame, charity and mercy were great and marvellous and his spirit was high, soaring, shining, as much as it could to prevent the assault of powerful enemies and cause delight to the world." This indicates that the divinity of Rāma Pāla was accepted by the people.

It may be argued that Sandhyākarananandin was a court poet and therefore his statements are not so reliable. A famous author of somewhat earlier date, Bāṇa, made an observation which shows that many kings received similar flattery.

1. *E.I.*, vol. 19, p. 58, *E.I.*, vol. 8, p. 141.
2. *Jiṣṇuṣucijīviteśakatānidhikamaleśapavanadhanadevam* ।
Yaur vedhā vyadhita Samāhāraṁ kila Lokapātānaṃ ॥ 16 ॥
R.C., p. 13.

He stated[1] : "Thus are kings deceived with more than mortal praises by men ready to raise faults to the grade of virtues, practised in deception, laughing in their hearts utterly villainous; and thus these monarchy by reason of their senselessness, have their minds intoxicated by the pride of wealth and have a settled false conceit in them that these kings are really so; though subject to mortal conditions, they look on themselves as alighted on earth as divine beings with a superhuman destiny, they employ a pomp in their understanding only fit for Gods, and win the contempt of all mankind. They welcome this deception of themselves by their followers. From the delusion as to their own divinity established in their minds, they are overthrown by false ideas and think their own pair of arms have received another pair, they imagine their forehead has a third eye burried in the skin. They consider the sight of themselves a favour; they esteem their glance a benefit; they regard their words as present; they hold their command a glorious boon; they deem their touch a punishment." This passage suggests that the doctrine of the divinity of kingship was a means of gaining favour; and that the king in allowing himself to be addressed by divine title was a victim of flatterers. Bāṇa[2], however, was an author with a particularly individual mind, when allowance is made for his time and place. His own real views on the royal divinity may have been critical, but a latter passage of the same work shows that he was quite used to such flattery; for one of his characters is made to say[3] : "Therefore, the birth of Gods among mortals is not hard of belief, And thou, Sire, art not behind the men of old in virtue, nor is the moon greater than the God from the lotus springs." This gives the impression that Bāṇa himself thought the incarnation of a God as a man was not an impossibility, and the spirit of the passage suggests that he himself would have addressed a king as a divine being. Moreover, the earlier passage of Bāṇa quoted above is a piece of advice given by a king to his son to avoid the flattery of the courtiers, and such advice cannot be accepted as indicating a view widely held in the courts of our period. It may be suggested that the writings of great authors

---

1. *Kim bahu Hariravatīrṇah sa yaśodānandayorucitram* l
Prandhāri Vāri jagadānandakamudyadvirājidhạmāsya l|19ll *R.C.*, p. 15.
2. *Kādambarī.*, p. 84 (Ridding's version).
3. *Kādambarī*, p. 201.

reflect the spirit of times. The people called the king divine, so, though aware of the hollowness of the royal divinity. Bāṇa also addressed the king as divine, as we have seen in the second quotation from the *Kādambarī.* Besides this there are many examples in dramas and stories of courtiers addressing the king as *Deva*, meaning God, as Bāṇa himself depicts in the case of Harśavardhana[1] of Kanauj.

The divinity of kingship was accepted by Merutuṅgācārya.[2] Like Lakṣmīdhara he believed that the prosperity of the people was dependent upon the merit of the king. He illustrated his views in a story which runs as follows—One king Vikramāditya of Ujjain went to the chief courtesan of the city and asked her for a drink. Then a procuress went to bring some sugar-cane juice for the king. She crushed the sugar-cane, but the juice derived from it was just half of the normal amount. She came back and gave it to the king. Having drunk the juice, the king enquired the reason why it was so little. In course of discussion the procuress replied that the king's mind was set against the people. Therefore, even the moisture of the land was drying up. That ideas such as this were current evidently proves that the king was thought of as divine. If the king had not been thought divine, the procuress would have given some other scientific reason.

In another place Merutuṇgācārya referred to the king as a manifestation of the Gods. He stated[3] : "In the city of Kānyakubja, the royal residence, which is of the size of thirty-six lakhs of villages, the king Bhudeva fell in love with the wife of the servant who superintended the beverages of the king and caught hold of her in his arms. Then the lady replied 'O Lord ! you are manifestation of all the Gods, why do you show your passion for a low woman ?" This is a statement that clearly shows belief in the king's divinity.

---

1. *Deva sarvasyāsya vindhyasya svānū sarvapaltīpatīnām* l
prāgrahar̥ śaharasanāpatirphūkampo ñama ll
H.C., ch. viii, p. 232, f, etc.

2. *Veśyāpi vadat pr̥thvipater manaḥ prajāsu virrudham Jātam tatah* l
pr̥thvīrasopi-kṣino jataḥ l *Iti kārṇaṃ nivaditavartī* ll
P.C., p. 8.

3. *Nr̥pena ca tatrāgatene bāhudaṇḍe dhr̥tā sati sā tam bhupamavādit svāmin* l
sarvadevatāvatārasya bhavato hanta ko' yam nīcanānjamabhilāṣaḥ ll
P.C., p. 11.

Kalhaṇa is another authority who, inspite of being extremely critical of many of Kashmir kings, accepted the divinity of many of them. Finally we have an authority who was not only an author but a king also. This is Harṣavardhana of Kanauj, who is said to have been a great scholar and author of the famous dramas as *Ratnāvali*, *Priyadarśikā*, and *Nagānanda*, In the *Ratnāvali*, he not only accepts the divinity of kings but makes his characters worship the king as God.[1] This suggests that the kings were not merely satisfied with being called divine but they also encouraged the people to worship them in a godly manner.

Hence, we may conclude that though different doctrines on the origin of kingship were maintained in different schools and sects, divinity of kingship was accepted by all in the India of our period. It must be remembered, however, that in ancient India divinity was believed to be widespread in many persons or objects, as it is believed to be today by the uneducated Hindu Brāhmaṇas and ascetics were also divine, and the king's divinity evidently did not make him infallible.

---

1. *Vāsavadattā nāṭyena rājānāṃ pūjayati* ll *Ratnāvali*, p. 30.

Chapter IV

CHARACTER OF KINGSHIP

Prof. Dikshitar[1] and several other scholars, taking the word *Rājan* as based on the root *rañj*, upon the authority of the *Mahābhārata* and the *Digha Nikāya* story, hold that the institution of kingship was thought to be established in order to please the people, and that this function of the king was always prominent in Hindu India. The quotations cited from the *Mahābhārata* or from the *Dīgha Nikāya* certainly give the impression that by performing the royal duties honestly, the king gladdens his subjects, but this has an altogether different implication than that read into the stories by Prof. Dikshitar. We have seen in the last chapter that according to most traditions there was anarchy at the beginning of creation. It was believed that the unjust dominated the just, and it was the oppression and high handedness of the unjust that brought the institution of kingship into being. To stop the evils caused by the misdeeds of the unjust a number of royal duties was prescribed, by performing which the king was expected to relieve the people from their troubles. On the other hand none of the texts known to us favours slackness in the administration to please people. The *Matsya Purāṇa* states[2] that the mild king cannot attain the superior rank. The *Mahā Purāṇa*[3] stated that it was very essential for the king to be severe, because only when people were afraid of the king's severity, they would perform their respective duties properly. Śukra held that the king is the cause of time and of good practices. By a terrible use of his engine of sovereignty he should maintain the subjects each in his proper sphere.[4] Thus all these texts urged the king to be stern and advised him to adopt any administrative measure, however rigorous, for the sake of good government. At the same time king Lalitāditya Muktāpīḍa of Kashmir, according to Kalhaṇa,

1. *H.A.I.*, p. 56.
2. *Mat. Purāṇa*, ch. 220, vols. 21-22.
3. *M.P.*, vol. 1, ch. 16, vols. 253, p. 369.
4. *Śukra*, ch. 1, v. 119-120.

is said to have communicated the rules of government to his son Kuvalayāditya in these terms[1] : "Those who wish to be powerful in this land must always guard against internal dissension. Because of foreign enemies (*paraloka*) they are as little in fear as the cāravākas of the world beyond (*paraloka*). Those who dwell in the mountains difficult to access, should be punished, even if they give no offence; because, sheltered by their fastnesses they are difficult to break up if they have (once) accumulated wealth. Every care should be taken that there should not be left with the villagers more food supply than required for a year's consumption nor more often than wanted for (the tillage of) their fields. Because if they should keep more wealth they would become in a single year very formidable Ḍāmaras and strong enough to neglect the commands of the king." The passage in question suggests a very stern government, a government which was not prepared to allow people on the road to prosperity from the fear that they would grow too strong and overthrow the regime. So every measure was to be applied by the king to keep the people under control. Strikingly enough, this passage is attributed to Lalitāditya, one of the most famous and most benevolent kings of Kashmir.[3] Rulers with such an attitude towards the ruled could not claim that the king's function was to please the people. Therefore, it seems better and more reasonable to derive the word *rājan* from the root *rāj*, an assumption that has been propounded by Prof. H. Shastri in his commentary upon the *Amarakoṣa*[2] of Amara Siṃha. This root may mean the rule, to govern, to be king, etc. Rājan is in fact an Indo-European word, and there were *Rājas* even when the Aryans invaded India.

We have several passages which suggest that the king was meant to rule rather than to please or shine ; for example the *Mahā Purāṇa* stated that Vṛṣabhadeva did not receive orders from anybody, but superior to Indra, Sun & Moon, being seated in the throne, he ruled this earth surrounded by oceans.[3] Bhoja of Dhāra states that the glory of the city of Ayodhyā was due to the royal command of the legendary king Raghu, by whose orders demon were driven out.[4] Nayacandra Sūri states that

1. *Rājā.*, ch. 4, v. 345-348.
2. *Amarakoṣa*, Edited by H. Shastri, p. 267.
3. *M. Purāṇa.*, ch. 16, p. 372.
4. *Campūrāmāyana*, p. 3.

the Rājput chief Cāhamāna rose in power to rule because "having obtained the paramount power from the fourfaced creator, he ruled over the heads of mountain."[1] The above quotations point to the conclusion that the king's commands were thought of as divine, and were to be followed without any opposition. There was to be no obstruction in the way of his administration, and all others were to accept the suzerainty of the king. Passages of this type suggest that the absolute form of monarchy prevailed in our period.

But before we accept absolute monarchy as the prevailing form of government for our period we have to consider the factors that made the monarchs absolute. The first source of his power appears to be the hereditary right of the king to the throne. This is a subject of some controversy, because a scholar of the importance of R.C. Majumdar[2] has suggested that the elective principle had not completely vanished even in our period and quoted the authority of Hiuen-Tsiang to show that Harṣavardhaṇa was elected to the throne of Kanauj. Undoubtedly there is reference in Hiuen-Tsiang[3] to this effect, but it is difficult to derive any general conclusion from this passage. Grahavarman, the last Maukhari king of Kanauj, had been killed without leaving an heir, and there is no reference anywhere to the existence of a claimant to the throne from within the Maukhari family. Harṣa, as the liberator of Kanauj, was in a very strong position and already *de facto* control. It would in any case have been difficult to prevent his accession. Moreover, it was only Bhaṇḍi and other officials who decided to invite Harṣavardhana to occupy the throne of Kanauj. These officials, as far as we can gather, neither were the representatives of the people nor did they consult the people about the appointment of the new king. According to Hiuen-Tsiang their decision was couched merely in the form of a resolution, and the final decision placed in the hands of Harṣavardhana alone; we are told that these officials said to Harṣa, "We pray you not to reject our proposal" which implies that Harṣa could have turned down the resolution if he wished to do so, and suggest the invitation of a council of regency rather than anything

1. *H. Mahākāvya*, I. p. 2.
2. *Corporate Life in Ancient India*, p. 112.
3. *Buddhist Record of the Western World*, vol. 1, p. 211.

like a constitutional election. Had it been a popular election we should expect Harṣa to have been told that his accession to the throne was at the wish of the people, and that the people wanted him to be their ruler. Finally, we are told that Harṣa did not come to the throne merely at the request of the royal officials. Before deciding he went to the Bodhisattva Avalokiteśvara for advice, who advised him to accept the throne, but not the royal title. Thus, if we are to believe Hiuen-Tsiang's story, it was the divine Bodhisattva who brought Harṣa on the throne ; the Chinese account may be based on a popular Buddhist belief, heard by Hiuen-Tsiang, that Harṣa came to power with the consent and encouragement of a Buddhist divinity.

In fact Bāṇa and Harṣa's own inscriptions do not suggest that he had great interest in Buddhism in the early part of his reign. The invitation to accept the throne of Kanauj, which was engineered by his cousin and general Bhaṇḍi, was evidently a formality, legalizing what had already in fact come about through a combination of various circumstances.

The Khalimpur copper plate[1] inscription of Dharmapāla is another record that has been taken by almost every Indian authority to show that the popular election of the king sometimes occurred in ancient India. But the epigraph in question states that Gopāla was brought to the throne by the *prakṛtis*. The word *prakṛti* does not normally mean the people; Kauṭilya used it in the sense of minister: *Prakṛti* was used in the sense of ministers by the Kashmiri poet Kalhaṇa, who stated about Yuddhiṣṭhira I that "His *prakṛtis* did not accept the conciliation (offered) by him, thinking : "He has seen our guilt; when he has recovered his position he will undoubtedly destroy us."[2] Thus we see that the word *prakṛti* is indicative of minister in these places. On the other hand there are several references to the effect that, in case of failure of heirs, the ministers proved very influential in the appointment of a new sovereign, as was the case with Meghavāhana of Kashmir[3] who was approached by the ministers of Kashmir and agreed to be their ruler. Similarly we have seen that after the death of Grahavarman,

1. *E.I.*, vol. iv, p. 248.
2. *Rāja.*, ch. I, v. 365.
3. *Rāja.*, ch. III, v. 2.

ministers of the kingdom approached Harṣavardhana to be their ruler, and Harṣa accepted the invitation.[1] Thus we see that these appointments were made at the ministerial level. As the ministers were in no sense the representatives of the people so the appointment made by them cannot be accepted as the popular appointment of the king. Furthermore, there were several rulers in the Pāla dynasty after the death of Gopāla, but none of them claimed to be elected by the people. Therefore Prof. Majumdar's assumption that there were certain survival of elective monarchy has no real basis as far as our period is concerned.

On the other hand Caṇḍeśvara lays down the order of royal succession thus :—That the ruler should be succeeded by his eldest son; in the absence of the eldest son he should be succeeded by the eldest son of the eldest son, if the eldest son died leaving no heir to the throne, the younger son of the king should succeed. If the king has no younger son in that case the nearest relative of the king should be brought to the throne.[2] Śukra[3] speaks of the royal succession in the following manner :—If in the king's family there be many males, the eldest among them is to succeed. If the eldest son, however, is deaf, leprous, dumb, blind or a eunuch he will not be eligible for the throne; in this case the king's brother or his eldest son's son should succeed. If these heirs are dead or ineligible the eldest sons' junior (i.e. the king's second son) or the son of the same king's brother should get the throne. In the absence of the seniors the juniors are the heirs to the throne. At present we are not concerned with the question as to how far these rules were followed in our period but it is clear from these quotations that it was considered that the throne should normally be inherited by a prince of the royal blood, and that in the absence of such an heir by the nearest relative of the dead king. Kāmandaka[4] held that a king should crown a son of his own, graced with good manners, as his successor. The *Matsya*[5] *Purāṇa* contains the story of king Yayāti, who, by setting aside the

1. *Buddhist Record of the Western World*, vol. 1, p. 211.
2. *R.N.*, p. 73.
3. *Śukra.*, 1, v. 784-690.
4. *Kām.*, ch. 7, ver. 6.
5. *Mat.*, 34, v. 24-25.

rights of the elder son, brought Puru to the throne. The decision made by the king was challenged by the people on the ground that Turvasu was the legal heir to the throne. But king Yayāti overruled the public protest, quoting the authority of the sage Śukra that only that son deserve the throne who obeys the king, which suggests that not only hereditary succession by primogeniture was usual, but also that the king's will might have some effect in bringing his favourite son to the throne even when he was not the eldest. There is a similar story in the Jaina *Mahā Purāṇa*[1], where it is stated that king Śrīseṇa of Videha, having set aside his eldest son's right to the throne, crowned his younger son Śrīvarman. This again proves the king's great influence in the selection of his heir.

Now let us see how the royal succession worked in practice. Jaitrā Siṃha,[2] finding that his sons were able to relieve him of the burden of government, one day talked over the matter with Hammīra, and after giving him advice how he was to behave, gave over the charge of the kingdom to him and himself went to the forest. From this account we find that the throne was regarded as hereditary, and nobody but the old king had any say in the appointment of a new one. Jaitrā had many sons and all of them were capable of holding the throne. But it was Hammīra whom the ruling king wanted to succeed, and hence he advised him on the principles of kingship, and not the others. The person to be consulted was the royal successor himself and nobody else. Jaitrā had a horde of councillors and royal officers, but as far as we can gather, he neither consulted them nor even mentioned anything in advance about his retirement to them. The text is silent about the councillors' advice to the new king on the complesities of the day-to day affairs of the kingdom. It was the old king himself who advised the successors and made him accept the throne. Thus it was the desire and decision of the Jaitradeva alone that brought Hammīra to the throne. Merutungācārya makes a reference to the Paramāra king Simhadatta[3] as setting aside the legal right of his own son Sindhala and placing his adopted son Muñja on the throne. The same source gives the information that

1. *M. Puraṇa.*, 5, v. 207, p. 112.
2. *H. Mahākāvya.*, v., 55-56, p. 65 ff.
3. *P.C.*, p. 21.

Cāmuṇḍarāj was succeeded by his younger brother Durlabharāja.[1] These references suggest that rulers were free to nominate their own successors, but the royal successor was selected from the nearest relatives of the king. Hence we see that kingship was hereditary and nobody but the old king had any say in the appointment of the new one. Thus it was that rulers came to power and claimed the divinity to which we have referred to earlier.

Prof. Dikshitar and others have accepted the fact that kingship was hereditary, but think that the office of the kingship was the creation of the people and the king held the throne conditionally, i.e., under certain terms. Any violation of the terms would lead to the banishment or deposition of the king. But Prof. Dikshitar has not defined these terms in his book, and none are to be found in any literature of the times. None of the sources, belonging to our period, refers to coronation oaths such as those taken by the ruler of the Vedic period or kings of the western world. Therefore, we are not sure as to what Prof. Dikshitar meant by those definite terms. It may be that he implied frequently repeated general principles on the proper performance of the royal duties by the king, but we shall see in the next chapter that, though many rulers were negligent in their duties, none of them were constitutionally replaced by more efficient rulers. The example given by Prof. Dikshitar[2] of the Śiṣunāga dynasty and Mahāpadma Nanda are quite unconvincing, because neither of these kings were brought to power with the consent of the people nor by constitutional means; according to all sources they were usurpers. Moreover, they existed long before the period we are discussing, when conditions were very different. In any case as far as the historical evidence goes we do not find any trace of popular rebellion in their regimes. Both dynasties came to power by usurpation, and both became victims of further usurpation. On the other hand, the tyrannical rule of king like Harṣa of Kashmir and other kings of the mediaeval period, as we shall see later, was patiently tolerated by their humble subjects.

Mr. J.N. Sammadar[3] has raised an interesting point in this connection. He stated that : "There was a controlling

1. *P.C.*, p. 20.
2. *H.A.I.*, p. 68.
3. *J.B.O.R.*, vol. 6, p. 521.

agency, no matter the extent of the control which was exercised must have varied in different times. It does not matter whether it was banishment or punishment on this side of the world or the threat of the hell, or the coronation oath which controlled, but the king was never above the law." Prof. Dikshitar[1] stated that with law above the king, and the *Paura Janapada*, the council etc. by his side, the king could not dream of an autocratic form of government. "He has quoted a verse from the Kaūtilya *Arthaśāstra* suggesting the importance of the people in ancient Indian Monarchy. But the quotation from the *Arthaśāstra* needs re-examination. The passage in question does not give any conclusive idea of the nature of kingship. It vaguely states that on account of the anger of *prakṛtis*, it is heard that several kings were killed. The first thing to be noticed in this connection is the use of the word *prakṛtis*. It was the *prakṛtis* who killed these kings. We have seen earlier in this chapter that *prakṛti* does not necessarily mean the people, but in many cases is used in the sense of the ministers. If the word *prakṛti* is accepted as meaning ministers then we find records of several rulers being killed by them, such as Nāgānanda of the Śiśūnāga dynasty and Bṛhadartha, the last of the Mauryas. We have no evidence that any of these regicide ministers has as their motive the good of the people. They appear primarily to have acted for their own benefit. Puṣyamitra, the slayer of Bṛhadartha, established the Śunga dynasty, the murderer of Śiśunāga king Nāgadasaka set up the Nanda dynasty, and the minister of Kashmir brought to the throne a king of their own choice, who continued to rule on the lines adopted by the previous rulers. Therefore, such rebels must not be regarded as acting for the public benefit. The ministers regularly acted in the interest of the people in checking the king's policy is by no means proved. The ministers were in no sense representatives of the people, and in the best known example of ministerial opposition to the king, that is recorded in the Girnar inscription of Rudradāman, the ministers opposed the king when he planned something of public benefit. The qualification of such ministers were their wealth, loyalty and intellect. A man brought up in opulence is usually unsuccessful

1. *H.A.I.*, p. 76.

in understanding the troubles of the poorer people who constitute the majority of the population of a territory. There may have been ministers who opposed the king, but their number was probably limited. Most of the sources belonging to our period advised kings to choose their own supporters as ministers and friends. Kāmandaka stated that "a monarch should appoint his kinsman of tested fidelity in the important offices.[1] Śukra[2] stated that the king's kinsmen were to act as his councillors. The *Matsya Purúṇa*[3] held that the royal officers must not oppose the wicked deeds of the king. Reference from these texts suggests that kings normally had either their own men or obedient ministers in their council. In such cases vigorous oppostion in the popular interest from the ministers' side appears to be improbable, to say the least. Moreover, the *Agni Pūrāṇa*[4] stated that "The king should not trust one and the same minister in all matters on all occasions. He should take councels with many but follow the decision of a single minister." This suggest that the council of ministers had little or no voice in the formation of the policy of the kingdom. It was only one minister whose advice was to be accepted by the king, and even that single minister, whom the king might consult on certain occasions, was not to be trusted to all times. Thus on different occasions different ministers were consulted. So it appears that rulers generally mistrusted their ministers. Therefore, in order to secure the king's trust and favour, ministers would not have regularly opposed the king. Caṇḍeśvara held that on affairs of administration first of all the king should consult his ministers himself and decide on his own what steps should be taken.[5] Here we again find that the ultimate decision lay with the king and not with the ministers. Therefore, it appears very hard to believe that the ministers, opposition would have carried much weight in the day-to-day administration of the kingdom.

Thus the *Mahā Purāṇa* states that king Mahābala used to take decisions himself for the administration of the kingdom and

1. *Kām.*, 5, v. 74.
2. *Śukra.*, 1, v. 686.
3. *Mat.*, ch. 216, v. 16.
4. *Agni.*, ch. 225, v. 20.
5. *R.N.*, p. 10.

his ministers merely approved and appreciated them.[1] King Muñja[2] disobeyed his ministers, advice and waged war at his own initiative. Writing about king Durlabhaka Pratāpāditya II of Kashmir, Kalhaṇa[3] reported that he was not instructed by his ministers, but guided his ministers who merely carried out the policy laid out by the king. In another place Kalhaṇa approved the attitude taken by Bijjā[4] in disobeying the councillor's advice, which gives the impression that in case of difference, rulers would overrule their ministers and act according to their own choice. One of the Cauhān chiefs Vira Nārāyaṇa,[5] neglected his ministers, advice and made a treaty with Alāuddīn, which brought about his end.

Thus our analysis shows that in most cases ministers were dependent upon the king for the formation of the policy of the kingdom, and when the policy was framed by the king, they would merely approve it and carry it out. This is quite contrary to the democratic ideals of government. Thus it appears very difficult to agree with the contentions of Prof. Dikshitar and others that monarchy in ancient India had any elements of democracy about it. On the other hand being absolute, the king may have been further encouraged to claim the divinity to which we have referred earlier.

Another important source of the king's absolute power was his great wealth. He was possessed of the whole land of his kingdom, as we shall show in the sixth chapter. Besides land, he had income from the mines, rivers, forests, mountains, etc. He used to receive taxes on meat, honey, ghee, medicine, perfume, flowers, roots, juice, vegetable,[6] etc., as well as his main tax on the products of the soil. Taxes from *bhikṣus*, widows and other means were also realised. For example Merutuṅgācārya[7] recorded in the story of Mayaṇallādevī, the mother of the Gujarat king Siddharāja, that *bhikṣus* coming from a far off land were not allowed to worship the God Śomesvara because they could not pay the religious tax called *pañcakula* to the tax collector,

1. *M. Purāṇa.*, ch. 4, vol. 195.
2. *P.C.*, p. 22.
3. *Rājā.*, 4, v. 51.
4. *Rājā.*, 7, v. 555.
5. *H.M.*, (introduction) p. 9.
6. *Kṛtya Kalpa.*, p. 90 ff.
7. *P.C.*, p. 57.

and thus they were insulted. In the *Rājataraṅgiṇī*[1] there is a reference to the king Śaṃkaravarman realising tax on goods produced for religious consumption. Hence we find that temples, brāhmaṇas, and religious bodies all paid taxes to the royal treasury.

Having thus secured enromous wealth at his disposal the king was in a position to meet all the effective financial demands made upon him, such as remuneration to scholars, construction of dams and canals, encouragement of foreign trade, etc., not to speak of maintaining the pomp and luxury of his court and supporting a large army for his military venture.

Both[2] Prof. Dikshitar and Altekar stated that kingship was regarded as trust. Prof. Altekar has quoted a passage from the *Agni Purāṇa* in favour of his statement. The text reads "A king should be delighted in the happiness of the people; he should behave like the expectant mother, who sacrifices her pleasure for the benefit of the child. The king has not been created for his own benefit but for the good of the people. Therefore, the king should not spend money for his own pleasure or that of the royal family. He should spend it for the protection of his army, his subjects and *dharma*. On the other hand, there are few references which go against the spirit of the statement in the *Agni Purāṇa*. Merutuṅgācārya[3] has presented a few significant stories of the reign of king Bhoja of Mālawā, one of which runs as follows :—"One fine morning, having considered the transitoriness of life and unsteadiness of property, Bhoja started to give gift of gold and *mohars* to petitioners. His minister named Rohaka, who had failed to stop the king's liberality, worte on the door of his council house 'save money for emergency'. Next morning the king came across this inscription and inquired from his people who had written it. When all refused to tell him he wrote back 'what misfortune for the fortunate ?' In answer to this the minister replied, 'what if ever fate grows angry ?' Then the king replied, "In that case even the savings will be destroyed.' Then the minister, being answerless, appeared and confessed that it was he who had written all these remarks. Thereafter, the king ordered brāhmaṇas to feast in his palace

1. *Rāj.*, ch. 5, v. 168.
2. *H.A.I.*, p. 77, *S.G.A.I.*, p. 65.
3. *P.C.*, pp. 25-26 ff.

regularly. Afterwards[1] the king put on a bracelet, engraved with the four principles of his life. So long as there is wealth do good to others. Otherwise one would not get chance to do so on the eve of the misfortune which is bound to come (II) O full moon ! gladden the world with moonlight, otherwise you would not get time to do so because the God will not permit the immortality of human beings. (III) O lake ! this is the time to serve others by day and night, (IV) O river ! the eroder of the trees, the flood of water will not stay very long, but the erosion of the trees shall remain for ever. Furthermore I do not know what I shall do with the wealth that is not distributed by sunset." The same author presented another story of ordinary folk[2] who were starving for days before they met the king. The family had no proper clothing even during the peak of the Indian winter during the reign of the same king Bhoja. Then it appears, while the people were suffering from bad times, the king instead of taking any preventive measures to stop people's starvation, continued to earn righteousness by distributing his gold *mohars* to petitioners. There are a number of kings recorded as spending money lavishly in our period. We can take king Ananta of Kashmir[3] as one such example. This king allowed the trainer of his horses to plunder the kingdom, and let his favourite Dallaka loot the people because he was a clever jester.

Besides these it has been reported in the Kashmir Chronicle that only the king's favourites were appointed in the royal treasury. The Hammīra Mahākāvya[4] informs that the Kothārī (incharge of the royal treasury) tried to please Hammīra by giving him a false account of the hoarded property it contained. In these circumstances it appears that the real master of the treasury was the king himself, and that the *Bhāṇḍāgārika* and other royal officers usually tried to please the king by allowing him to spend as much as he liked. Thus, being the supreme authority over the royal treasury of the kingdom, rulers of the period spent money as they chose.

Having considered the king's power over the country's finance let us see what authority the king enjoyed in the sphere

1. *P.C.*, p. 29.
2. *P. C.*, p. 29.
3. *Rāja.*, ch. 5, v. 166 onwards.
4. *H.M.*, ch. 13, v. 136 onwards.

of law. Here we find almost every *Smṛti* author and commentator stating that the law is devinely ordained and that the king is appointed only to decide law suits, not to make new law.[1] Prof. Laski has made a very good comment upon such traditions of devinely ordained law—a summary of which would not be out of place since it is largely applicable to the India of our period. He remarks[2] that such laws are framed and obedience is demanded to them in the name of God. The virtue of society lies in its following them, and disobedience to them brings the fear of the anger of heaven upon society. These people have to follow the laws which they did not make from their own practical experience. Such laws lack the human approach and often prove very troublesome to the people in general. They ignore the dynamic changes of a society where institutions and human customs are out-dated sooner or later.

Almost every source belonging to our period stated that law was divinely ordained. On the other hand we have seen that the *kulakaras*[3] are said by the Jainas to have started all institutions in India. It makes us believe that it was probably the intelligentsia of the time, chiefly represented by the brāhmaṇas, who framed the Hindu law in the name of the Gods—brāhmaṇas particularly, because it was chiefly they who were encouraged to read and think. The legal traditions of Hindu India were in fact framed over a long period chiefly by brāhmaṇas acting mainly in the interests of the ruling classes, and using as their main raw material local religious tradition and customs, which were sanctified by the claim to a divine origin for them. They reserved most of the rights in their own favour and placed the king at the head of the law, so that they could derive most benefit out of it.

Many authors of the period declared in varying term that the people in the absence of law and order would fall into a state of anarchy where the stronger devours the weaker and the just suffers at the hands of unjust. But people are frightened of a king who is possessed of the rod of the justice and only thus do they follow their respective duties. Hence the king with the rod of justice in his hands is able to rule over the world. Nārada[4]

1. *Nārada*, ch. 1, vols. 21, *Medhātithi on Manu*, vii, v. 14 etc.
2. *An Introduction to Politics*, p. 23 ff.
3. *M. Purāṇa.*, 16, v. 252, 253.
4. *Nārada.*, 1, vol. 2.

held that "the practice of duty having died out among mankind, law-suits have been introduced; and the king has been appointed to decide law-suits, because he has authority to punish." Caṇḍeśvara,[1] quoting Manu, held that "For the king's sake the Lord formerly created his own son, punishment, the protector of all creature, an incarnation of law formed of the glory of brāhmaṇa. Through fear of him all created beings, the movable and immovable, allow themselves to be enjoyed and swerve not from their duties." Śukra[2] said: "The king should punish the wicked by administering justice." Medhātithi[3] commenting upon Manu held that : "As without punishment the king cannot carry on the work of protecting the people, it was for proper accomplishment of the kingly function that punishment was created. Thus we see that the king was placed at the head of the justice and Hindu philosophers advised him to enforce the rules that were imposed upon them by the Gods.

The *Matsya Purāṇa*[4] stated that a kṣatriya who abuses a brāhmaṇa should be fined 100 *paṇas*, a vaiśya doing so should be fined 200 *paṇas*, and a śudra should be sentenced to capital punishment. A brāhmaṇa who abuses a kṣatriya should be fined 50 *paṇas*, if he abuses a vaiśya he should be fined 25 *paṇas* if he abuses a śudra, the fine should be only 12 *paṇas*. A vaiśya abusing a kṣatriya should be fined the first amercement (*prathama sāhasa*), but if a śūdra abuses a kṣatriya his tongue should be cut out. If a kṣatriya abuses a vaiśya he should be fined 25 *paṇas*, and if he abuses a śūdra he should be fined 25 *paṇas*. If a śūdra abuses a vaiśya he should be fined 1080 *paṇas* but a vaiśya abusing a śūdra should be fined only 50 *paṇas*. A fine of a thousand *paṇas* was regarded as the first amercement, five hundred *paṇas* as the medium and two hundred and fifty *paṇas* as the lowest.[5] At present we are not concerned with the justification of this aspect of the Hindu Law, but have found sufficient evidence to show that the punishment differed for the same crime in different castes, and the nature and degree of the punishment was decided according to the superiority or

1. *R.N.*, p. 62.
2. *Śukra.*, iv. Sec. v. v. 1.
3. *Medhātithi on Manu*, vii, v. 14.
4. *Mat.*, 277, ver. 67-71.
5. *Manu.*, viii, v. 138.

inferiority of that caste. Thus Hindu monarchs maintained in their kingdoms unequal laws in the name of the Gods, which must have weighed heavily on the unprivileged castes.

Thus Hindu laws made in the name of Gods were so rigid that there was little room for the alteration according to the needs of the times. For example Aparārka[1] states that if there is contradiction between the *smṛtis* and *arthaśāstra* the precepts of the *smṛti* should be followed, because *arthaśāstra* is weaker, and if any body through the influence of *arthaśāstra* disobeys the laws of *dharmaśāstra* he will incur the sin of murdering a brāhmaṇa. The *Bhaviṣyat Purāṇa* states that the source of the *Smṛti* is *Veda*, therefore, *smṛti* laws must be followed. Thus on the one hand we find much emphasis laid upon the necessity of adherence of laws propounded in the *dharmaśāstra* literature, and on the other hand the disparagement of the *arthaśāstra* law, that may for fully have met the needs of the time than that of the *dharmaśāstra*. Adherence to the *arthaśāstra* was regarded as a heinous crime and those who did so were thought of as incurring the greatest sin possible. Thus we see how the dynamic force of society was neglected.

Now the question arises whether the king was a real source of justice, or whether this was just the contention of the Hindu theoreticians. Dr. Kane has quoted passages from different sources to show that rulers were the real heads of the judicial system of the country and performed their duties conscientiously. But there are references where kings are found working in defiance of the existing law. For example we may cite the case of the tanner given in the Kashmir Chronicle.[2] This man refused to give his house to Chandrāpīda for the construction of a temple. The tanner was rebuked and asked to appear in the royal court. He appeared, and king Candrāpīḍa welcomed him with the following words. "Why are you just obstructing my pious work ?" And the tanner replied, "O king, if I tell you something just as it is in my mind, then as a true judge, you should not stand by proudly. I am not less than a god, nor is the king greater than the descendant of Kākutstha. Why then should your courtiers seek, as it were, (the sight of) this

1. *Quoted by Aparārka*, p. 626.
2. *Rāja.*, iv. v. 66-67.

conversation between us.........As this palace resplendant with stucco is to your majesty, so to me is the hut in which the window is formed by the mouth of a pot. Since my birth, this hut has been to me like a mother, witness of good and evil days I cannot bear to see it being pulled down to-day. The misery which men (feel) when their homes are forcibly taken away could be described only by a God who has fallen from his celestial car or else a king who has lost his kingdom. Notwithstanding this, however, I should have to give it up if your majesty would come to my dwelling and ask for it in accordance with propriety." The story suggests that some kings were quite ready to confiscate the personal property of their subjects, and there was no higher court of justice in the kingdom where people might have appealed against the will of the king. Of course there is no substantial legal argument given by the tanner in the defence of his property; his arguments are sentimental and sentimental reason counts very little before justice. But this act of Candrāpīḍa was also in defiance of the *smṛti* law, for the *Nārada Smṛti* and others declared that the king should not interfere with the land occupied for habitation of the people.[1] Yet Candrāpīḍa did so because he had nobody to fear and was strong enough to ignore the pious injunctions of the sacred law. So he succeeded in dispossessing the poor man of the land where he was born and brought up, the land which he loved more than his mother. Merutuṅgācārya[2] has mentioned a similar incident of the biased justice of king Yogirāja of Gujarāta, who failed to punish his sons who had committed robbery with violence. There is a fictional incident to this effect mentioned by king Harṣa of Kanauj, who described how Jīmūtaketu was hesitant to deliver judgment upon his sons.

An analysis of the above facts shows that the rulers of the period were often the real authors of law, as well as the upholders of the divine law of the *arthaśāstra*. In most cases allegations brought against the members of the royal families and other favourites as well as in cases involving their own rights and interests, partiality was shown, and consequently the people suffered.

---

1. *Nārada.*, xi. 142.
2. *P.C.*, p. 14.

The power of the king also largely rested on his command of the royal army. Kāmandaka[1] advised the king to have a hereditary, well-disciplined, well-equipped and obedient army. Agreeing with the *Mahābhārata* Caṇḍeśvara[2] recommended the king to command the different branches of the army in person. Thus we find theoreticians urging the king to maintain a strong, well-equipped and loyal army under his own command. Hindu theoreticians were not merely satisfied with advising the king to take the command of the royal army in person, but they also urged him regularly to supervise military training and investigate the discipline deserved by the army. So they made it a part of the king's daily routine to supervise the army bases, accompanied by the commander-in-chief. The *Agni Purāṇa*[3] advised the king to inspect the army before his evening prayer. Aparārka[4] recommended him to visit the different wings of the army in the afternoon and according to Śukra[5] the king should spend one *muhūrta* over the military exercises of the regiment.

Writers of the period, such as Lakṣmīdhara[6] authorised the king to carry out military operation on his own initiative. He was expected to think over strategy personally and to devise means to subdue foreign kings. There is no reference whatsoever to the commander-in-chief or any other official or ministerial council waging war on their own initiative, and no minister of peace and war has been described as making peace with a foreign king without the king's permission. On the other hand the *Matsya Purāṇa*[7] stated that the king was entitled to take any measure to gain victory. Aparārka,[8] wanted the king to keep all military affairs in his own hands and himself decide the measures to be taken.

In practice we find that the king Ananta[9] of Kashmir led the royal army and fought against Tribhuvana who was once

1. *Kām.*, iv. v. 65-67.
2. *R.N.*, p. 34.
3. *Agni.*, 225, v. 14.
4. *Aparārka on Yāj.*, 1, v. 327.
5. *Śukra*, I, v. 567. 9.
6. *Kṛtyakalpa.*, p. 111.
7. *Mat.*, 223, v. 4-5.
8. *Yāj.*, 1, v. 327.
9. *Rājā.*, 7, ver. 155.

his powerful commander-in-chief. Hiuen-Tsiang[1] has presented an interesting account of the king Harṣa's expedition against Śaśāṇkarāja and other hostile kings in the following words : "Now he commanded his ministers saying 'the enemies of my brother are unpunished as yet, the neighbouring countries not brought to submission, while this is so my right hand shall never lift food to my mouth. Therefore, do you people and officers unite with one heart and put out your strength.'...Accordingly they assembled all the soldiers of the kingdom and surrounded the masters of the arms. They had a body of 50,000 elephants, a body of 20,000 cavalary, and 50,000 foot-soldiers. He went from east to west subduing all who were not obedient the elephants were not unharnessed nor the soldiers unbelted. After six years he had subdued the five Indies." Throughout the career of Hammīradeva[2] we find him planning military operations, and leading the army in person. King Muñja, in Merutuṅgācārya's *Prabandhacintāmaṇi*[3] is described as leading his army against the enemy. King Rāmapāla of the Pāla dynasty is described by Sandhyākara as leading an army against Bhīma, the kalacuri king in person and giving the enemy very close fighting. There are innumerable examples to this effect in the literature and inscriptions of the period.

Thus we see that the Indian kings commanded the army, prepared plans for military operations and fought against the enemy in person. The example of king Ananta suggests that even during the time of rebellion rulers used to go to war persanally and suppress the trouble caused by the insurgents. Thus it can be assumed that the king's command over the army was another factor leading to his absolute authority.

In addition to this another cause leading to the absolute authority of the king was the influential position in religious affairs. The *Matsya Purāṇa*[5] states that the king should propagate the study of the *Vedas* in his kingdom. The *Matsya Purāṇa*[6] states that the king should try to advance religion by following

1. *Buddhist Record of the Western World.*, vol. 1, p. 23.
2. *H.M.*, ix and onwards.
3. *P.C.*, 32, 22 etc.
4. *R.C.*, ch. 2, v. 8 onwards.
5. *Mat.*, ch. 215, vol. 65-67.
6. *M. Purāṇa.*, ch. 42, vol. 4 onwards.

religious customs acceptable to all. References to this effect are again many, and need not be counted here. We give, however, a fine example of kings who took the lead in the religious affairs of their kingdom.

We are informed by Kalhaṇa[1] that Meghavāhaṇa of Kashmir, soon after his initiation to the throne, proclaimed by the beat of drum that there should be no slaughter of living beings in his kingdom. Killing of animals stopped and butchers were paid from the royal treasury for their maintenance. The king's command was so strictly followed that people used to offer an effigy made of pastry in place of living animals on sacrificial occasions. This story of Meghavāhaṇa accords with many of the orders of Aśoka engraved in the rock inscriptions[2] where he is described as having stopped the killing of living beings in his palace and limiting their slaughter throughout his realm. There is a similar example in the case of Kumārapāla[3] of Gujarat. This pious Jaina king's policy is described by his teacher, Hemacandra, in the form of a prophesy put into the mouth of Mahāvīra himself. "Hunting, which even the Pāṇḍus and other pious kings did not give up, he will abjure, and all men will do likewise at his command. When he forbids all injury there will be no more hunting or other cruel sports. Even an untouchable will not kill a louse." King Siddharāja[4] of Gujarat has been described as the propagator of the *Śvetāmbara* sect of Jainism. All these stories suggest that the rulers of the period exercised power to maintain religion. But this attitude of the Indian kings does not appear to be beyond criticism because in many cases these rulers favoured that religion which they followed. Many people belonging to other religions must have been critical of the policies of the Jaina kings of Gujarat; many Śaivites believe in animal sacrifices and their sacred books encouraged them to perform such sacrifices. Therefore, the enforcement of the law of non-violence must have been very distressing to them, especially on ceremonial occasions, and might have resulted in communal disharmony.

Besides this, we have references to several kings of the

1. *Rāja.*, III, vol. 5-7.
2. *Rock Edict.* iv. *Girnar version* p. 7.
3. *Life of Hemacandrācārya.* p. 88.
4. *P.C.*, p. 68.

period who fought for the protection of religion. Dāhir of Sindhu[1] fought a religious war against the Arabs to save thousands of Hindus from being forcibly converted to Islam. King Anandapāla, when expecting an attack from Mahmūd of Gazni, appealed for aid to other Hindu Rājās. It is said that the Hindu kings complied with his appeal and the Rājā of Ujjain, Gwalior, Kālinjar, Kanauj, Delhi and Ajmer either marched to support him in person or sent their troops in his assistance.[2]

Many of the Pāla inscriptions of our period contain the word *Viniyuktaka*[3] who was probably a minister in charge of the religious and moral affairs of the kingdom. At least from Mauryan times the king often tried to maintain religion and morality with the help of special officials. "The *Samanamahāmātras* of the Sātavāhana period and the *Vinayasthitisthāpaka*[4] of the Gupta period appear to have been only the counterparts of the *Dharmamahāmātras* of the Aśokan period. This system of controlling religion was continued by the Hindu kings down to the Marathas of Tanjore. Thus we can say that the Indian rulers of our period tried to maintain and control religion by appointing a special minister for the purpose. Thus by defending religion from external intervention, checking unrighteousness by appointing a special minister, and encouraging the study of religion, rulers of the period may have established their supreme authority over the religious affairs of the kingdom and controlled religious activities.

Finally, the king's authority over society may have been an important factor contributing to his absolute power over his kingdom. Aparārka[5] held that the king should try to remove differences arising among the members of the different communities, and press them to follow the practices of their respective communities. The *Mārkaṇḍeya Purāṇa*[6] held that "A king's highest duty and that which brings felicity for him is the maintenance among men of their laws, since they are disturbed by

1. *Cambridge History of India*, vol. III, p. 5.
2. Ibid., p. 16.
3. *E.I.*, vol. iv. p. 253.
4. *Mahalingam, South Indian Polity*, p. 122.
5. *Aparārka on Yāj.*, II, 192.
6. *Mārk.*, ch. 27, ver. 30.

evil-minded men." Nārada[1] advised the king to maintain the usages of heretics, corporation, etc. He stated that whatever be their laws, their religious duties, the rules regarding their attendance and the particular mode of livelihood prescribed for them, those the king shall approve of. The king shall prevent them from undertaking such acts as would be either opposed to the wishes of the king or contemptible in their nature or injurious to his interests. Medhātithi[2], commenting upon Manu held that the king shall punish the breakers of contacts relating to villages and caste-federations. Such examples show that the king was entitled to interfere in purely social affairs such as the maintenance of caste solidarity and traditional practices. There are passages in early Indian literature where such corporations appear quite true from the fear of royal intervention. But the citations provided above clearly authorise the king to maintain control over them and to punish those who disobey the rules of the community.

The quotation from the *Nāradasmṛti* above gives the impression that people were dependent upon the king's approval even for the rules of their society, their religious practices, and their mode of life. The king was entitled to judge these things from his own point of view, and from the point of view of the safety of the kingdom. If their social practices, their mode of livelihood etc. seemed injurious either to the king or to the kingdom he had every right to stop them. Moreover, the king might in certain cases play a part in family and personal affairs; thus Nārada[3] observed that a maiden having no male relative to look after her may approach the king and the king should arrange for her marriage. Several references to this effect have been given by Merutuṅgācārya.[4]

This paternal attitude of the king towards his people, which we have already considered in an early chapter must have had influence in establishing the king's authority over the social affairs of the kingdom.

There is a reference in Kalhaṇa[5] that king Mihirkula slaughtered three thousand women of respectable births,

1. *Nārada.*, ch., x. v, 2-4.
2. *Medhātithi on Manu.*, vol., viii, v. 221.
3. *Nārada.*, ch. xii, v. 33.
4. *P.C.*, p. 9.
5. *Rāja.*, I, v. 318-319.

together with their husbands, brothers and sons for being unchaste. Talking about the reign of king Gopāditya[1] Kalhaṇa observes that "He removed those who ate garlic to Bhūkṣiravātika and transferred the brāhmaṇas who had broken the rule of their conduct to Khāsata; other brāhmaṇas again of a holy life, whom he had brought from pure countries, he settled in the Vāścika and other Agrahāras." The use of garlic, onions, etc., by higher castes was regarded as against the rules of society. Therefore, the king, as the head of the society, tried to keep it pure by removing *dvijātis* who were lax in this respect. Finally Sandhyākara Nandin[2] observes that "He (Lava as well as Madanapāla) being a friend of this world and causing Lakṣmī to bloom and enemies to fade, relief takes place, all sources of vices vanish and righteousness prevails", which again shows how the Hindu authors of the period looked on their kings as responsible for the maintenance of morals and the removal of evils from the society. Similar passages can be found in many sources of our period, both literary and epigraphic.

Thus by maintaining the morals of the people and keeping them obedient to their own laws the king added to his power in the eyes of his subjects and enjoyed almost absolute authority over them.

Hence, we see that the typical king of our period, having come to the throne by right of birth, ruled according to his own conscience and controlled the finance, army and judiciary of the kingdom. And finally, he exerted his superiority over the religious and social affairs of the kingdom. A monarch exercising all these powers at his own risk can rightly be called absolute, if we accept the characteristics of the absolute monarch as presented by Aristotle[3] that an "absolute monarch does everything according to his own will."

---

1. *Rāja.*, ch. 1, v. 342-343.
2. *R.C.*, ch. iv. v. 39.
3. *Politics*, Book III, ch. xvi, p. 100 ff. (Everyman's Library series).

Chapter V

THE ROYAL DUTIES

Almost all our sources assign numerous duties to the king and advise him to follow them literally; for instance Śukra[1] stated that the person who practises his duties and sticks to them can become powerful and influential in this world. The Jaina author Somadeva Sūri[2] pointed out that "The king is the maker of the age. When the king rightly protects his subjects all the quarters are wishing cows, Indra rains in due season, and living beings are at peace." The same view was held in south India. Thus the *Kural*, the famous collection of Tamil proverbs, declared[3] "Rain and plentiful crops will ever dwell together in the country of the king who sways his sceptre with justice; when there is rain the world enjoys prosperity; and when the king rules justly, his subjects prosper." Thus prosperity of the people was thought to be subject to the performance of the royal duties by the king. In case of the just performance of the royal duties the heavenly powers would bestow blessing on the land, and peace and prosperity would reign amongst the people. In case of the non-performance of the royal duties misfortune will fall upon the realm. This doctrine has nowhere been better expressed than in the Buddhist text *Suvarṇabhāsottama Sūtra*[4], which reads as follows:-

> "When the king disregards the evil done in his kingdom, and does not inflict just punishment upon criminals, unrighteousness quickly grows, and fraud and strife increases in his kingdom through his neglect of evil. Then the thirtythree great gods are angry in their palaces, as the king disregards the evil committed in his kingdom, and the land, afflicted with violent and terrible crimes, perishes, and

1. Yo hi svadharmaniratassa tejasvī bhavediha *Śukra*, i, 46.
2. *N.V.*, p. 183.
3. Quoted by T.V. Mahalingam in *South Indian Polity*, p. 22.
4. *S. Sūtra*, xii.

falls into the power of enemies. Property, families and wealth disappear, and men ruin one another with various deeds of deceit. If, for any reason, a king does not do his duty, he ruins his kingdom, like a large elephant (trampling on) a bed of lotuses.

Then fierce winds blow, and the rain does not fall in season. Planets, stars, moon and sun are unfavourable. If the king is negligent, corn, flowers, fruits and seed do not ripen properly, and there is famine.

Then the kings of the gods say to one another. 'This king is unrighteous, he has sided with unrighteousness ! 'So he will lose all he values at the hand of his brother or son. He will lose his wife, and his daughter will die. Fire will fall from heaven ..as fear of the enemy and hunger increase. His favourite minister will die and his favourite elephants, and one by one his favourite horses and camels...

There will be strife, violence and fraud in all the provinces, and calamity and terrible plague will afflict the land. Brāhmaṇas will be unrighteous and righteous men will be punished ...And where the wicked are honoured and the good are despised there will be famine, with thunderbolts and death All living beings will be ugly; they will have little vigour, and be very feeble. They will eat much, but not be filled; they will have no strength or varility all living things in the land will be lacking in vigour.

Many evils such as these befall the land where the king is unjust and disregards wicked deeds...But he who distinguishes good deeds from evil, and shows the results of *karma* (to his subjects) is called a true king. Ordained by the gods, the gods are pleased with him. For his own sake or the sake of others, in order to preserve the righteousness of his land and to suppress rogues and criminals in his domains such a king would abandon his life and his kingdom...but not the jewel of righteousness, whereby the world is gladdened."

It can be well imagined that crimes and evil deeds would grow in the land of the negligent king, but the displeasure of the gods that was thought to cause the destruction of his kingdom needs further consideration. This belief is apparently connected with the doctrine of the divinity of king. We have seen earlier that the king, being composed of particles of different gods, was created by the High God for the protection of the people, and not for his own pleasure. Therefore, it seems quite logical that in cases of the king's failure to perform the royal duties, these gods would withdraw the particles of their own essence from the king and cease to work for the benefit of his kingdom which would be ruinous for the king and his territory.

What were these royal duties on which the welfare of the nation depended ? In answer to this both Caṇḍeśvara and Lakṣmīdhara[1] agreeing with Manu, stated "Not to retreat from the battlefield, to protect the people, to honour the brāhmaṇas are the best means to secure happiness for the king." Thus, on the basis of this verse, the royal duties can be devided under three different heads : (1) military; (2) administrative; (3) and religious, and we shall consider the royal military duties first.

It is well known that there was no unified government of India in our period and the country was divided into several principalities. Each sovereign was inimical to the other and attempted to extend his own territory by annexing that of the other. As result of this, war between different sovereigns was very frequent, and must often have caused much distress among the general public. Therefore, the protection of the people from foreign aggression constituted one of the main functions of the king.

For the protection of the people against invasion the *Mahāpurāṇa* stated[2] that the king should settle his people in a place where there was no danger of aggression. Lakṣmīdhara[3] suggested that the king should construct different types of fortified places (for example, *giridurga*, defended by hills, *mahidurga*, defended by earth works, *dhanurdurga*, surrounded by desert, and *vana-durga* surrounded by forest) as a measure

1. Saṃgrāmeṣvanivarttitvaṃ prajānāṃ caiva pālanam l Śuśrūṣā Brāhmaṇānāṃ ca rājñāṃ śreyaskaraṃ param ll *R.N.*, p. 55 *Kṛtyakalpa*, p. 154.

2. *M.P.*, ch. 42, v. 161-162.

3. *Kṛtyakalpa.*, p. 39.

against foreign aggression for the protection of people, cattle and the treasury, because he realised that one bowman placed on a rampart was match in a battle for one hundred foes and one hundred for one thousand Caṇḍesvara[1] suggested that the royal capital and the houses of the citizens should be built within the sourrounding walls of the fortresses.

Medhātithi[2], commenting upon this as part of the royal duties, stated that : "Wherever the king is challenged he must fight, whoever the challenger may be (either a foreign sovereign or bandits), and he shall take no account of the caste or age or training or ambition of the other party. The king has to bear this duty always in his mind. In order to counteract the fear of death in battle the warrior dying in a fair fight was promised great rewards in the after life. Thus death on the battlefield was eulogised in the following words of Medhātithi :

> "It has been declared without any reservation that the sacrifice is immediately accomplished for the kṣatriya who is killed by means of uplifted weapons in due accordance with the duties of the kṣatriya, and again 'those two persons pierce through the solar orb—the renunciated in meditation and the hero killed in the forefront of the battle"—further in the *Mahābhārata* it has been declared that heaven is attained even by those who witness the battle.
>
> "The giving up of his life by the king for the benefit of the people is actually conducive to merit.
>
> "In the case where a king's realm is attacked and pillaged by another king, and his people are being massacred, if the former undertakes to fight against him and loses his life in the fray, this would be conducive to merit. If he does not fight, he falls into blind darkness, which means hell, on account of the total absence of light ......When a man has accepted service for pay under a master, if he fails to fight for his master in battle and abandons him, his fall into hell is certain. On the other hand if the man has fought his master's battle and has

1. *R.N.*, p. 26.
2. Medhātithi on *Manu.*, vii, v. 89.

become free from the debt of the wages which he has received from him—if he is not bowed down by his sin—it is natural that he should attain heaven, by virtue of his own meritorious acts. It is in view of this that it has been declared that his sacrifice becomes immediately accomplished......

Every warrior was not killed in the battlefield, but it was to be expected that many of them would be wounded. Therefore, the *Mahāpurāṇa* stated[1] that the king should protect his troops wounded in the battlefield by employing experienced doctors and giving them proper treatment. After their recovery the king was expected to see to their maintenance. In case of dead soldiers the king was advised to appoint their sons and brothers to their posts. Śukra[2] held the same view.

It is beyond objection that Hindu rulers normally paid every attention to the protection of the people against external aggressions. There are innumerable examples to support this statement, and it is needless to mention them here. But it would not be unreasonable to conclude this section with a few observations from the reports of foreign travellers of the period. Al-Masūdī[3] wrote : "The king of Kanauj has four armies according to the four quarters of the wind. Each of them numbers—7,00,000 or 9,00,000 men. The army of the north wars against the prince of Mūltān and with the Mussalmāns his subjects on the frontier. The army of the south fights against the Balahara king of Mankir. The other two armies march to meet enemies in every direction." This king of Kanuj referred to by Al-Masūdī has been identified by R.S. Tripathi[4] with the Pratihāra king—Mahīpāla I, and the Balahara with the Rāṣṭrakūṭa king of Mālkhed. It is clear from the statement of Al-Masūdī that the danger of the invasion of Kanauj from different points was realised. So Mahīpāla divided his army into different commands and stationed them in various strategic areas, so that they might

1. *M.P.*, ch. 42, v. 148.
2. *Śukra*, ii, v. 832-833.
3. *History of India*, vol. 1. p. 23 (by E.&D.)
4. *History of Kanauj*, p. 266.

always be ready for the battlefield without undertaking the trouble of general mobilisation from one end of the country to another in order to resist the enemy effectively. Sulaiman the Merchant[1], who come to India during the time of Bhoja I of the Pratihāra dynasty, observed : "I have never seen the people of one country submit to the authority of another". These two famous foreign accounts of the period show that Indians were not prepared to tolerate any foreign infringement of their territory, for the defence of which they employed large armies and offered every possible resistance to the aggressors.

It is very difficult to discover what was done for the families of deceased or disabled soldiers, because none of the sources of our period give any direct evidence on the matter; but some sources do suggest that proper care and treatment were offered to the wounded soldiers. We are told that Jayasiṁha[2] of Kashmir spent a huge amount of the royal income on the marching allowances and medical treatment of his soldiers. It appears from the description of Chandbardāī[3] that doctors were employed for the medical treatment of the wounded soldiers in the royal court of Pṛthvīrāja.

But it was not always the external foes who were sources of public trouble. There were wicked people within the king's dominion, such as thieves, robbers, murderers, etc. against whom the people needed protection. Caṇḍeśvara condemned[4] the deeds of the *cāṭas*, thieves, seducers and murderers, and held that the very existence of these people endangered the security of public property and the welfare of the populace in general. The interpretation of the word *cāṭa* is controversial. Mr. Balgangadhar Sastri took the word as meaning the royal favourites, while Prof. Bühler[5] gave it the meaning of the irregular troops. Dr. Fleet[6] accepted Prof. Bühler's interpretation and translated it in the sense of irregular

1. *History of India*, by Elliot and Dowson, vol. i, p. 7.
2. *Rāja.*, viii, 740.
3. *P. R.*, p. 276.
4. Cāṭataskaradurvṛttamahāsāhasikādibhih l Pīḍyamānāḥ prajā rakṣetkāyasthaiśca viśeṣataḥ l *R.N.*, p. 54.
5. Quoted by Prof. Bühler in *Indian Antiquary*, vol. 5, p. 115.
6. *Gupta Inscriptions*, p. 98.

troops in many of the inscriptions edited by him. Prof. Vogel[1] took the modern word *cāra*, still used in Camba in the meaning of a district officer, as the corrupt form of *cāta*. Prof. Bühler's interpretation has been accepted by many modern historians of ancient India, while Vogel's interpretation seems equally difficult to refute, because in many of the inscriptions[2] *cāṭas*, followed by *bhaṭas*, are found among the names of the royal officers who are forbidden to enter granted villages. But Caṇḍeśvara[3] evidently interpreted the word in a rather different sense. He took it as meaning an evil-minded person and stated that *cāṭas* are oppressors. Aparārka[4] commenting upon Yājñavalkya, held that the king should protect his people from *cāṭas* and other trouble makers; he further commented upon the word and stated that *cāṭas* are *piśuṇāh*, meaning backbiters, informers, or betrayers. At the same time the word *cāṭa* was used along with words meaning thieves, robbers and other similar criminals by several other authors of the period. Therefore, it seems that whatever may have been their real character and whether they were in the king's service or not *cāṭas* were trouble makers and were subject of the hatred of the people in general. Disturbances caused by such anti-social elements had become so frequent in our period that the great Chinese traveller Hiuen-Tsiang[5] was robbed thrice while in India, and once even his life was imperilled by bandits in the neighbourhood of Ayodhyā and Kumāralabdha. The misdeeds of such criminals made Medhātithi say : "When robbers and others, in sheer disregard for established law, attack the people—or join the king's enemies if such persons cannot be subdued without war then the king must go to war against them, even though they be very week"[6]. From such passages as these it may be inferred that bands of robbers infested the land and often compelled the king to take large-scale military measures to suppress them.

1. *Antiquities of Champā State*, pp. 130 ff.
2. *G.I.* vol. xiv. p. 329, vol. xv, p. 29.
3. Cāṭaḥ pratārakaḥ
   R.N., p. 54.
4. Aparārka on *Yājnavalkya*, i, 334.
5. *Beal's Life of Hiuen Tsiang*, pp. 87, 200.
6. Medhātithi on *Manu*, vii, 87.

The *Agni Purāṇa*[1] stated that the king should protect his people against the extortions and oppressions of royal officers, favourites and *kāyasthas*. Kāmandaka held that the subjects had reasons to fear the *āyuktakas*, royal favourites, and similar people[2]. The reasons for protection against the royal officers are given by Caṇḍeśvara[3], who declared that the royal officers who are appointed for the protection of the people were liable to become knaves and seize property belonging to others. In the *Kathāsarit-Sāgara* we are told of the Prime Minister Guṇavarman plotting against the sovereign.[4] There are clear examples of corrupt royal officers in the chronicle of Kalhaṇa[5]; for instance he tells the story of a scribe during the reign of Yaśaskara (A.D. 939—948), who was bribed to falsify a deed in order to dispossess an innocent merchant of his belongings. In another place, writing about the reign of Jayasiṃha, Kalhaṇa reported that even Chief Councillor Somakāla of Loharā was prepared to accept bribes and desert his master.

Hindu theorists made it a part of the king's duty to extend protection to refugees and distressed persons in need of asylum. Bṛhaspati[6] stated that the king should protect the refugee from another country though guilty of all crimes. The king should welcome brāhmaṇas, kṣatriyas, princes and feudatories belonging to other countries with viands, clothing etc. as if they were of his own kingdom. In the *Mārkaṇḍeya Purāṇa*[7] we find a king saying to a Brāhmaṇa : "My duty is to protect those who have sought refuge with me". The *Matsya Purāṇa*[8] held the same view. This implies that the king, without considering the good or bad qualities of the refugee, was expected to give asylum to those who needed it.

---

1. Agni, ch. 223. Bhakṣyamāṇāḥ prajā rakṣyāḥ kāyasthiaiśca viśeṣataḥ Rakṣitā tadabhayebhyastu rājño bhavati sā prajā ll v. 12.
2. Āyuktakebhyaścorebhyaḥ parebhyorāja-vallabhāt, Pṛthvī-pati-lobhācca prajānāṃ pañcadhā bhayam. Kām., v. 82, 83.
3. *R.N.*, p. 54.
4. *Kathā.* p.
5. *Rāja*, 6, 41; *Rāj.* 8, v. 850.
6. *Br. Arth.*, ch. iii, 51-52.
7. *Mārk.*, ch. 131, v. 32,
8. *Mat.* ch. 215, 63.

The king's administrative function does not end here. The sphere of his duty extended beyond the protection of his subjects from evil-doers, to protect those whose troubles were caused not by others but by famine, disease, infirmity and other natural cause. Kāmandaka[1] held that it was the king's duty to take steps to counteract natural calamities such as pestilences, and try to promote his people's prosperity. Bṛhaspati[2] held that the king should take steps to encourage good agriculture. The *Mahā purāṇa*[3] declared that the king should provide good seed for the peasants and cause them to grow good crops; this text thus goes even further than famine relief and advocates a positive agricultural policy on the part of the king.

Besides these duties the king had certain defensive functions to perform towards the royal family and himself. Caṇḍeśvara[4] stated that the king should always try to defend himself against any infliction or injury to be caused to him. And the *Mahā purāṇa*[5] stated that by following a policy acceptable to the royal family the king should protect his *kula* or family. Moreover Śukra[6] stated that the king should bring up the royal children under favourable circumstances.

How far these duties were performed in practice is a matter of controversy. Profs. Kane, Bhandarkar, Altekar[7] and several others have stated that almost all these duties were performed by the Indian kings. We cannot say anything with cetainty about the performance of the royal duties towards the royal families, because almost all available sources were either written by court poets or by royal favourites, and as these people would not dare to displease the king by stating unvarnished facts, their accounts are not very dependable, and thus our knowledge of the matter is almost non-existent. Pro-

1. *Kām.*, iv, 54-56.
2. *Br. Arth.* ii, 4.
3. Tathā bhūpo pyatandrālurbhaktagrāmeṣu kārayet l Kṛṣiṃ karmāntikairbījāpradānādyair upakramaiḥ ll
M. P., 42, 176.
4. *R.N.*, p. 56.
5. *M.P.*, ch. 42, v. 4.
6. *Śukra*, ii, 43-46.
7. *H.D.S.*, iii, 60; *A.H.P.*, p. 190 ff;
S.G.A.I., p. 36 ff.

ceeding to the royal duties of putting criminals under check we have references to the effect that some kings, such as Harṣa[1] of Kanauj and Yaśaskara[2] of Kashmir, tried to maintain efficiently law and order throughout their kingdom. But during the reign of the same Harṣa of Kanauj[3], as we have pointed out earlier, the Chinese traveller Hiuen Tsiang was plundered and once even his life was in danger. Merutuṅgācārya[4] mentioned in one of his stories that the country of Gujarata during the reign of Vanarāja was known as the place of robbers. Finally, Vanarāja's own sons participated in plundering a vessel which had anchored in a Gujarat port because of rough weather, and Vanarāja killed himself by fasting to death instead of punishing his sons for their misconduct. Hence it appears that the administration was in many cases so weak and the laws were so mild that even the royal princes committed crimes.

Similarly the students find it hard to gather sound evidence that the king regularly protected the people against the oppression of the royal favourites. King Prabhākaravardhana[5] some time before his death, told his sons Rājyavardhana and Harṣavardhana that nearly all his royal officers were untrustworthy and oppressively high-handed. But Prabhākaravardhana is nowhere referred to as having taken any measures against such officers, though we are told that he appointed tutors of of his children from noble families, who were not even touched by the very existenee of corruption. According to Kalhaṇa king Yaśaskara[6] of Kashmir found out the misconduct of a royal scribe, who for a bribe tried to dispossess a merchant of his belongings; thereupon he exiled the defendant who had bribed the scribe and handed over his property to the plaintiff, but he is not recorded as having taken any steps against the scribe, who was expected to be upright and serve the cause of justice honestly. Besides this we are told of another Kashmir

1. *Buddhist Records of the Western World*, vol. i. p. 221.
2. *Rāja.*, vi, 41 and onwards.
3. Supra
4. *P.C.*, p. 14.
5. *H.C.* iv, 119. (Cowell's translation)
6. *Rāja.* vi, 38-41.

king, Pārtha[1], who appointed only those officers as councillors etc. who brought more and more money into the royal treasury at the cost of the poor peasants. Harṣa of Kashmir[2] tormented the country by employing *kāyasthas* in his service. It may be objected that almost all rulers employed *kāyasthas* or members of the class of scribes and so Harṣa did not make an objectionable innovation, by appointing these *kāyasthas*. *Kāyasthas* as a class cannot be condemned, and as citizens they were also entitled to positions in the royals ervice. But the word *kāyasthas* seems in Kashmir and elsewhere to have taken on the secondary meaning of a petty official, and such *kāyasthas* had the universal reputation of being oppressors of the people. Oppressors of the people, according to the spirit of all the texts on government, were not to be appointed in the royal service. But the appointment of such people to higher position in the government suggests that the kings were not always very solicitous for the protection of the people againsts the oppressions of the royal servants. Therefore, though Kalhaṇa's statement that Cakravarman[3] of Kashmir (A.D.936) appointed thieves and robbers in the government offices appears to be figurative, it must have some truth in it, and implies that the kings were not very strict towards their servants; consequently dishonest and extortionate servants continued to rob the people.

It would be very rashly imaginative to state on the strength of such texts as the *Mahā Purāṇa* that rulers of the period regularly carried out a positive agricultural policy by distributing good seeds among their subjects and performing other beneficient acts, because none of the sources refers to specific instance of this happening. We have, however, references to to the effect that there were certain kings who constructed dams and canals and embarked on similar enterprises to irrigate the cultivatable land. Bhoja, the eleventh century Paramāra king, appears to have been an energetic builder of reservoirs for irrigation.[4] Ajayapāla[5] of Cambā, Bhānudeva[6]

---

1. *Rāja.*, v, 275.
2. *Rāja.*, vii, 1226.
3. *Rāj.*, v. 391.
4. *I.A.*, xvii, pp, 350-2.
5. *A.C.*; i. p. 237.
6. *E.I.*, ix. p. 125.

of the Kankara inscription of Central India, and Rāmapāla[1] of the Pāla dynasty are all recorded as having constructed dams, canals, etc. for the public benefit. King Avantivarman[2] of Kashmir took every trouble to dam the river Jhelum and drain the flood water for the benefit of the people. But these benevolent rulers appear to be exceptional and comparatively rare, and there are many records to the opposite effect. Thus we are told of a king like Pārtha[3] of Kashmir, during whose reign famine befell the land, and who, instead of trying to relieve the sufferings of the people, realised taxes even when hundreds and thousands of his subjects were dying from starvation and various diseases. Merutuṅgācārya[4] has recorded a story of the reign of Sidharāja of Gujarāt, whose officers realised revenue even when there is famine in the country and people were starving. Had these rulers any desire to promote the prosperity of the people in their minds, they would certainly have refrained from realising taxes in the troubled days and arranged for relief.

The protection of refugees appears to have been undertaken by several rulers of the period. Thus we have references to king Ananta[5] of Kashmir, who offered refuge to the Śāhi princes after they had been expelled from their kingdom by the Muslim invaders, and who is said to have spent a huge amount of money in caring for their welfare. The famous Kashmiri poet Bilhaṇa, when exiled from his home-land was offered asylum in the Cālukya court.[6] This offering of asylum must often have had political significance; we are told that Hammīradeva[7] offered refuge to the Mongol chief Mahimā Śāhi who had fled to him from the tyranny of 'Alāuddīn. In course of time this Mahimā Śāhi is said to have become the most faithful general of Hammīradeva, the Cauhān chief. It seems that Mahimā Śāhi gave the secrets of Alāuddīn to

1. *R.C.*, iii, 42, p. 108.
2. *Rāja.*, v. 109. onwards.
3. *Rāja.*, v. 270-8.
4. *P.C.*, p. 96.
5. *Rāja.*, vii, 144.
6. *Vikramāṅkadevacarita* (Introduction)
7. *H.M.*, (Introduction), p. 9.

Hammīra, and the king, being pleased with his deeds and honesty, appointed him to a high post; no Hindu political thinker would advise any king to appoint a foreigner to such a responsible post. Candbardāī has recorded a similar story to the effect that Pṛthvīrāja[1], the Cauhān chief, offered asylum to the Muslim chief Mīr Hussein, who communicated to him the secrets of Muhammad Ghorī. He in his turn was appointed as the general of the Rājput army, fought against his old master, and gave the enemy a crushing defeat. The examples cited above imply that by offering asylum political motives were often served, and so for this reason, if for no other, rulers of the period would offer shelter to influential foreigners. When there were no political motives to be served rulers probably often failed to give asylum; thus it is said that king Visaladeva[2], one of the ancestors of Pṛthvīrāja did not offer refuge to any one and amassed wealth in his treasury instead of spending it on refugees.

It is hardly likely that refugees of the humbler classes were given much help. The *Lekhamālā*, a text giving specimens of legal documents from mediaeval Gujarat, quotes a contract of slavery signed by a girl of ten who has been driven from her homeland by the Muslim invasions and is forced to sell herself into servitude owing to destitution.[3]

Thus we see that administrative functions of king as laid down in the texts were not regularly carried out as fully as might be expected.

Next we consider the religious duties of the king. Bṛhaspati[4] stated that king should restrain people indulging in unrighteouseness. Kāmandaka[5] stated that "suppression of wrong and following the path of rectitude, and doing good to one who does good to him—these are the functions of the ruler of the earth." The *Mārkaṇḍeya Purāṇa*[6] stated that "The king who brings back to the pale of their own religion those foolish

1. *P.R.*, p. 389.
2. *P.R.*, p. 58.
3. Quoted by Majumder in *Cālukyas of Gujarat*, p. 347.
4. *Br.* Ar., ii, 68.
5. *Kām.*, viii, 58.
6. *Mārk.*, vvvii, 28.

persons who stay away from right paths and fall off from their duties, goes to the celestial region." Thus it was one of the king's duties to lead people along the path of the rectitude.

A further religious duty was thought to be performance of the sacrifices for the public benefit. For instance, the *Matsya Purāna* stated[1] that "a sovereign who has the well-being of the people at heart should always perform *gṛha-yajña* and *lakṣahoma*. Śukra[2] stated that the *rājasūya* and other sacrifices should be performed for the general benefit of the kingdom. Thus the performance of different kinds of sacrifices constituted another religious function of the king. Besides this the *Mārkaṇḍeya Purāna*[3] stated that the king should worship ascetics as gods and receive the boon of matchless sovereignty from them.

Both[4] the *Mārkanḍeya Purāṇa* and the *Matsya Purāṇa* stated that the king should make donations to religious causes. There is no reason to doubt that donations were to be made to the brāhmaṇas, but it may be asked who amongst the brāhmaṇas should receive the gifts. Prof. Kane[5], on the authority of Āpastamba and other sources, holds that it was only the learned brāhmaṇas who were eligible for the gifts. Manu, Yājñavalkya and other authorities have certainly made statements to this effect, but the unlearned brāmaṇas were by no means excluded from the list of the recipients. Gautama[6] stated that a gift to learned brāhmaṇas would bring several times the righteousness, and a gift to unlearned brāhmaṇas would also bring twice the righteousness obtained by giving gifts to the ordinary people. Caṇḍeśvara[7], agreeing with Manu, stated : "A gift to one who is not a brāhmaṇa yields the ordinary rewards, a gift to one who calls himself a brāhmaṇa a double reward, a gift to a well-read brāhmaṇa a hundred thousand times the reward and a gift to one who

1. *Mat.* ch. 232, v. 7.
2. Yajanaṃ rājasūyādeḥ kośānāṃ nyāyato' rjanam l *Śukra*, i. 246.
3. *Mārk.*, ch. 18, 57-58.
4. *Mārk.*, vii. 18; *Mat. P.*, 215, 56.
5. *H.D.S.*, vol. ii, part i, p. 112.
6. *Gautama*, v. 18.
7. *R.N.*, p. 15.

knows the *Vedas* and the *Aṅgas a* reward without end." Medhātithi[1], commenting upon Manu, held the same view. Thus from the statement of these sources it appears that there was variance in the amount of righteousness to be gained by giving gifts to learned or unlearned brāhmaṇas, but that learned brāhamaṇas were far more worthy recipients, from the religious point of view, than ordinary people. Therefore every brāhmaṇa was eligible to receive gifts.

Not only was the king expected to make liberal gifts to brāhmaṇas, but he was also instructed to serve them in various ways, an aspect of the king's duties especially emphasized by Caṇḍeśvara[2] and Lakṣmīdhara[3]. Just as he was advised to make gifts to all brāhmaṇas, whether learned or not, so the king was expected to serve all brāhmaṇas, though no doubt the learned had some preference. We have no evidence stating positively that only the learned brāhmaṇas should be honoured. In the *Mārkaṇḍeya Purāṇa*,[4] king Hariścandra, replying to a question of Viśvāmitra, stated : "I must always give gift to the brāhmaṇas". Bṛhaspati[5] states that if the king is approached by *dvijas*, he shall bow his head. These two examples imply that the king, without making any distinction between the learned and the unlearned, was expected to give gifts to the brāhmaṇas and treat them with reverence. From the study of the *Matsya Purāṇa*[6] and the *smṛti* literature it appears that the whole of the brāhmaṇa community was privileged, in comparison with the other castes, in the sphere of justice. Finally, Medhātithi[7], commenting upon Manu, stated: "Towards all brāhmaṇas he shall be tolerant, i.e. even when they have committed an offence punishment shall be meted out to them in a merciful and not in a revengeful spirit." Thus we see that brāhmaṇas as a community were specially favoured by the king.

Next to this comes the royal duty of the protection of the

---

1. Medhātithi *on Manu,* vii, 85.
2. *R.N.*, p. 55.
3. *Kṛtyakalpa.*, p. 154.
4. *Mārk.*, 7, 19-20.
5. *Br.* Ar. i, 69.
6. *Mat.*, 227, 66-68.
7. Medhātithi on *Manu,* vii, 32.

Varṇāśramadharma. This duty was looked on as primary by many sources. The *Mārkaṇḍeya Purāṇa*[1] stated that : "He in whose kingdom the duty of the four *varṇas* and the four periods of the brāhmāṇa's life does not fall in confusion, has eternal happiness after death and in the future". The *Matsya Purāṇa*[2] stated that in time of trouble "the king should provide for grains, utensils, oil, etc. etc. for the benefit of all the *varṇas*". The fact that *varṇas* are here specifically mentioned seems to imply that the motive was not so much the material welfare of the king's subject as the prevention of confusion of class functions as a result of hardship.

All *varṇas* had their own duties to perform. The study of the *Vedas*, offering or promoting sacrifices, and giving gifts were said to be the duties absolutely enjoined on thə brāhamaṇas, kṣatriyas and vaiśyas respectively, while each of these had certain further special activities such as teaching the *Vedas*, officiating at the sacrifices, and receiving of gifts for brāhmaṇas, the profession of arms and protection of the people for kṣatriyas, trade and agriculture for the vaiśyas, and the rendering of services to the twice-born for śūdras. So by enjoying the protection of the *cāturvarṇya* it was implied that the king should keep each *varṇa* within its own duty. From the above quoted passage of the *Matsya Purāṇa* it may be deduced that even in abnormal conditions each *varṇa* was expected to follow its peculiar duties. But this was not always the case in practice. Hindu thinkers appear to have been aware of the situation and important authorities such as Śāṅkhalikhita[3] and Aparārka allowed people to follow the means of livelihood prescribed for *varṇas* which was immediately below them, in days of distress, although people belonging to a lower caste might not legitimately follow the profession peculiar to the higher caste.[4] But soon after the end of the

---

1. *Mārk*., 27 28.
2. *Mat*. ch. 215, 64-65.
3. Āpatkāle mātāpitṛmato bahubhṛtyasyānantarakā vṛttiriti kalpaḥ l .... Tasyānantarakā vṛttiḥ kṣātro'bhiniveśaḥ l Trayāṇāṃ brāhmaṇa karmaṇāṃ yā vṛttiryājanādhyāpanapratigrahāṇāmevamapyajīvanvaiśyamupajivet ll Śāṇ.
   quoted by Aparārka on Yāj., iii, p. 930.
4. Na kathaṃcana kurvīta brāhmaṇaḥ vārṣalam l Vṛṣalaḥ karma vā brāhmaṃ patanīye hi te tayoḥ ll *Nārada, ṛṇādāna*, 57.

period of distress, those who have temporarily abandoned their caste duties were expected to perform penance and give up the wealth acquired by those abnormal means[1]. Another aspect of maintaining *varṇāśramadharma* was the prevention of inter-caste marriage, which was thought to incur the highest sin. The *Āpastamba Smṛti*[2] held that by marrying a girl of another caste a man incurred the highest sin and had to undergo penance. The legendary king Nabhāga[3], according to the *Mārkaṇḍeya Purāṇa*, married a vaiśya girl, incurred sin, and was turned off the throne by the divine sage Parivrata and his father Diṣṭhi. The same was the case with inter-caste dining. In earlier days there were no restrictions of this kind, but the *smṛti* authors are hesitant in permitting the acceptance of food from other castes. In the *Āngirasa Smṛti*[4] it is held that a brāhmaṇa may eat at a brāhmaṇa's table at all times, at a kṣatriya's only on festivals, at a vaiśyas when he is initiated for a sacrifice but at a śūdra's never, and the text adds that the food of the four *varṇas* are like nectar, milk, mere food, and blood respectively. In the latter law digests regulations on inter-dining were much elaborated.

There were several other complications of the *varṇāśrama-dharma* which need not be considered here because we are not directly concerned with them. But according to the *Dharma-śāstras* the king was expected to take care that every complicated rule was observed to keep the people confined to their own *varṇa*.

After these duties comes the royal duty of the protection of widows and minors.[5] The position of the widows in Hindu

---

1. Manu, xi, 192-3, Yāj., iii, 357, *Nārada, ṛṇādāna*, 57.

2. *Āpastamba Smṛti*, quoted in the *H.D.S.*, vol. ii, Part i, p. 451.

3. *Mārk.*, 113, 36.

4. Brāhamaṇasya sadā bnuṅkte kṣatriyasya tu parvaṇi l Vaiśyasya yajñadīkṣāyām śūdrasya na kadācana ll Amṛtaṃ brāhamaṇasyānnaṃ kṣatriyasya payaḥ smṛtam l Vaiśyasyāpyannavānnaṃ śūdrasya rudhiraṃ smṛtam l *Aṅgirasa*, 77-78, quoted in H.D.S., Vol. ii, Part ii, p. 790.

5. Sampādya rūpasaṅkhyādīnsvāmī taddravyamarhati ll
Bāladāyādikamṛkthaṃ tāvadrājā'nupālayet ll 18 ll
Yāvatsyātsa samāvṛtau yāvadvā'tītaśavaḥ l
Bālaputrāsu caivaṃ syādrakṣaṇaṃ niṣkulāsu ca ll 19 ll
Pativratāsu ca strīṣu vidhavāsvāturāsu ca l
Agni, ch. 223 Mat., ch. 215.

society was miserable. They were looked upon as inauspicious and so could not take part in any festivities such as marriage, or in similar other functions. They had to lead a life of celibacy, and even child widows were expected to live like ascetics, being poorly fed and poorly clad. Their rights to property were negligible. In early days a widow had no right to succeed to her deceased husband's property, but coming to our period we find that certain authors such as Kātyāyana, Aparārka and others allowed the widow the right of succession under certain conditions: "A sonless widow preserving the bed of her husband (unsullied) as residing with her elders and being self-controlled (or forbearing) should enjoy (her husband's property) till her death; after her the (other) heirs (of the husband) would get it".[1]

In connection with the performance of the religious duties of the king, we are told about several philosophical discussions in the royal courts; for example when Hiuen-Tsiang[2] arrived in India he had to participate in several such discussions, and he reported how king Harṣa of Kanauj arranged a discussion in his capital. There is a similar reference in the *Mahāpurāṇa*[3] to a religious discussion at the court of king Videha, where the ministers themselves are depicted as supporting some views and refuting others. Merutuṅgācārya[4] has recorded several stories of philosophical discussions in royal courts, in order to convince his readers that Jainism was the best religion.

We may raise an interesting problem here. Scholars such as Prof. Altekar have contended that religious tolerance prevailed in ancient India, and every religion had opportunity to prosper. There is nothing to make us doubt that Harṣavardhana of Kanauj patronized followers of all religions. The Muslim historian Awfi[5] recorded that Siddharāja, the

---

1. Aputrā śayanaṃ bhartuḥ pālayantī gurau sthitā l
Bhuñjitāmaraṇātkṣāntā dāyādā ūrdhvamāpnuyuḥ ll *Kāt.*, 921.
2. Also *Aparārka on Yāj.*, ii, 135.
2. *Life of Hiuen Tsiang*, iv, 176-7 (Beal's tran.)
3. *M.P.*, ch. v., 28-29 and onwards.
4. *P.C.*, 62.
5. *History of India*, vol. ii, p. 163-4.

Caulukya king, punished his Hindu subjects of Cambay for rioting against the Muslims and gave the Muslim merchant community funds to rebuild their mosque which had been destroyed in the riots. Al-Masudi[1] observed about the Balahara king (Amoghavarṣa Rāṣṭrakūṭa) that of all kings of Sind and India there was no one who paid greater respect to Musalmāns than Balahara. In his kingdom Islam was honoured and protected. But there are a number of cases of persecution by fanatic kings of sects of which they disapproved. Thus Śaśāṅka, a śaivite king, persecuted Buddhists and burnt the sacred Bodhi tree.[2] Sulaiman the Merchant[3] noticed of king Mihira Bhoja that "among the princes of India and Sind there was no greater foe of Islām than the prince of Jurz", which implies that Prof. Altekar's generalization was not universally true and that religious tolerance depended to some extent upon the character of the sovereign.

In Kalhaṇa there are numerous references to kings causing temples to be built. Thus Lalitāditya Muktāpīḍa[4] erected the shrine of Āditya at Lalitapura and Jayāpīḍa constructed the shrine of Vipuleśvara. There are so many epigraphic records of kings erecting temples that it seems unnecessary to give examples of them.

Not only were temples constructed but grants were also made for the running of the temples. Lalitāditya Muktāpīḍa[5] granted Kānyakubja to the shrine of Āditya of Lalitapura. Āsata[6] of Camba state granted an *agrahāra* to the God Viṣṇu. Here again the inscriptional records are very numerous.

There are several examples both from epigraphic and literary sources to show that most of the rulers of the period performed religious sacrifices, though there may have been a few kings such as Harṣa of Kashmir who, instead of offering sacrifices to the gods, established the office of *Devotpātanayaka* whose function was to look after the demolition of the temples[7],

1. *History of India*, vol. i, p. 24 (Elliot and Dawson)
2. *Buddhists Records of the Western World*, vol. ii. p. 122.
3. *History of India*, vol. i, p. 6 (Elliot and Dowson)
4. *Rāja* iv 189.
5. *Rāja* iv. 189 onwards.
6. *A.C.*, vol. i, p. 194, line 21.
7. *Rāja*, vii. 1091.

But in general even oppressive kings showed outward signs of piety. Bāṇa has presented a very good picture of the royal worship of Śiva by Prabhākaravardhana[1] of Thānesar. Hiuen Tsiang[2] observed the elaborate preparations and fasting preliminary to the worship of the gods by king Bhāskaravarman of Assam. We even find king Kalaśa of Kashmir, a thoroughly licentious character, offering sacrifice to Śiva. Thus it is evident that in most cases rulers performed religious sacrifices.

Rulers of the period appear to have been courteous and loyal to the ascetics. Hiuen Tsiang[3], in the course of his records, tells us how king Brahmadatta, having heard the arrival of a famous *ṛṣi*, went himself to meet and salute him, and thus addressed him graciously, 'Great *Ṛṣi* ! You are reposing in peace—what has disturbed you ?' Having heard the *ṛṣi*'s reason for coming, he tried his best to fulfil the *ṛṣi*'s wishes. This tradition recorded by the Chinese pilgrim shows how deeply engrained was reverence for the Hindu ascetics even in the Buddhist circles. Mūlarāja[4] and several other rulers of Gujarat are said to have paid the highest honour to the Jaina *sādhus*. Harṣavardhana[5] of Kanauj paid similar respect to the sage Divākaramitra and other Buddhist monks. There are so many examples of king's making gifts to brāhmaṇas and other religious sects from the beginning of Indian History to our period and it is needless to count them here. The legendary king Nahuṣa[6] married a vaiśya girl in violation of the *varnāśramadharma*. Merutuṅgācārya[7] informed us of king Āśarāja of Gujarat, who, being a kṣatriya, married a brāhmaṇa girl named Kumāradevī. Finally, we may conclude with the remarks of Śaṅkarācārya[8], who stated that *varṇāśramadharma* had become disorganised. This implies that kings did not care much for the performance of this function,

1. *H. C.*, iii, p. 85 (Cowell's trans.)
2. *Life of Hiuen Tsiang*, Book v. p. 172 Beal's Trans.)
3. *Buddhist Records of the Western World*, vol. i, p. 208.
4. *Prabhākara-carita*, p.p. 162-3.
5. *H.C.*, viii, p. 237 (Cowell's trans.)
6. *Mārk.*, 18, 57.
7. *P.C.*, p. p. 98.
8. *Vedānta sūtra*. i, 3, 33, quoted in H.D.S., vol. ii, part 1, p. 61.

which was one of the main duties of the king according to orthodox teaching.

The royal attitude towards the widows and minors appears often to have been unsatisfactory. King Āśarāja of Gujarāt is said to have married a widow against her will in order to procure mighty sons.[1] Kalhaṇa[2] appears to have been annoyed at the attitude of some kings towards widows and remarked about the dissolute Kalaśa that in his cruelty he disregarded all the rules of conduct and went so far as to seize the property of those who died issueless. Widows were the legal heirs to their husband's separate property in our period[3]. So any confiscation of her property would be regarded as an act of injustice. Thus it is clear that rulers of the period often failed to maintain their duties in order to satisfy their greed and lust.

On many occasions kings are described as dishonouring Gods and brāhmaṇas, for example, Tārāpīḍa of Kashmir[4], who is said to have hated the Gods, punished the brāhmaṇas, thinking that through their spells they cause the power of the Gods to be present. A brāhmaṇa Vararuci, a court *paṇḍita* of Vikramāditya, is said by Merutuṅgācārya to have been insulted by a royal princess[5]. But on the whole it appears that brāhmaṇas as a community were respected and honoured by the rulers of the period. As an example we may quote Bāṇa[6], who stated that the brāhmaṇas themselves thought of king Harṣavardhana as their ready servant. In a stone inscription[7] of the eleventh century from Govindapur in Central India it is recorded that a certain brāhmaṇa, even though he was not possessed of the requisites of wisdom sufficient to hold any responsible post, was appointed as the chamberlain of the Māna king ; this is an indication of the lengths to which a king's patronage of brāhmaṇas might sometimes go.

---

1. *P.C.*, p. 98.
2. *Rāja*, vii, v. 697.
3. Supra, p. 103.
4. *Rāja.*, ch. iv, 122.
5. P.C., P.4.
6. *H. C.*, ii, p. 63.
7. *E. I.*, vol. ii, p. 339.

Thus we may summarize our conclusions on the performances of the royal duties by stating that the king's religious duties were carried out fairly adequately according to the standards laid down in the *smṛtis*, but there were certain exceptions, for some of the rulers, being proud of their power and position, did not care to fulfil their duties and neglected those who ought to have been respected. As far as the king's administrative functions are concerned we feel justified in stating without prejudice that most rulers of our period were either comparatively inefficient or proved themselves total failures, when judged by the standards of the political literature of the time.

Profs. Kane, Dikshitar, Altekar, Pannikkar and others held that in cases of failure in performance of the royal duties, or in cases of justified discontent, the people were morally and legally entitled to revolt against the ruling authorities, and several Sanskṛta passages have been quoted in favour of this argument.[1]

There is a reference to the same effect in the Kashmir chronicle where it is stated that king Yudhiṣṭhira[2] was overthrown by the *prakṛtis*, because he failed to bring about the prosperity of the people. The author of the text has used the word *prakṛti* to describe those who overthrew Yudhiṣṭhira, and, as we have considered earlier, that word normally stands for ministers and similar royal functionaries rather than the subjects in general. Thus we cannot admit that it was the people who overthrew Yudhiṣṭhira. This king, moreover, belongs to the early period, which is to be thought of as legend rather than history, and therefore he does not deserve much of our attention. On the other hand, in the Kashmir chronicle[3] there are numerous examples of kings, for example Pārtha, Harṣa and others, who were negligent of their duties and oppressed the people by realising exorbitant taxes even in the days of dearth and starvation. But nowhere are

1. *H.D.S.*, vol, iii, p. 26, *H.A.I.*, p. 73, *Bhāratīya Vidyā*, vol. ix, p. 3, *J.D.D.*, (Calcutta University), vol. iii, p. 312, Rājadha p. 179., Origin and Evolution of Kingship, P. 33.
2. *Rāja.*, ii, concluding portion.
3. *Rāja.*, v. 274., *Rāja.*, vii, 1085 onwards.

we told about any popular revolt that these tyrannical rulers had to face. We are informed of a popular uprising during the reign of Cauhān king Visaldeva[1] against his misconduct and bad rule. But this story, occurring as it does in a Rajput legend, may well be an exaggeration, because the same king is described as ruling after the revolt and carrying on the same course of misconduct, thus if any revolt took place it was a total failure. There are several descriptions of the general discontent in the writings of Merutuṅgācārya[2]; for example he tells us that Sindhula, one of the favouriter of king Muñjarāja of Gujarāt, tortured an oil presser in ordes to extort his property from him; there is a similar reference in a latter portion of the book, where king Siddharāja[3] of Gujarāt is said to have killed the Rāṇā of Saurāṣṭra without any good reason. Finally we are told about the Cauhān chief Hammīradeva, who is said to have tyrannized over his people, realising heavy taxes at the instigation of his blind minister[4]. Yet we find no traces whatever of revolt against the king, who is depicted as a great hero and a martyr to Hindu freedom, second only to Pṛthvirāja in the Rājput tradition.

Hence we may conclude that though theoreticians usually agreed that popular revolt was justified in cases of bad rule and general discontent, we do not find any trace of such popular revolt in practice. Therefore, it would not be unreasonable to conclude that kings, being, fearless of popular opposition, ruled according to their own wishes and paid little, if any, attention to public opinion.

---

1. *P.R.*, 85.
2. *P.C.*, p. 21.
3. *P.C.*, p. 65.
4. *H.M.*, Introduction, p. 31.

Chapter VI

THE KING AND THE OWNERSHIP OF LAND

The ultimate ownership of land in early mediaeval India is a very debatable subject. Indologists have gone to much trouble to show that the private ownership of land was prevalent in our period. But the examination of their arguments suggests that facts have been distorted and points have been misrepresented. Therefore, we attempt to consider those facts and to throw some new light upon the topic.

Prof. Dikshitar,[1] relying upon the authority of Dr. K.P. Jayaswal,[2] tried to establish the existence of individual ownership of land in ancient India. But the validity of Dr. Jayaswal's theory has been challenged by Prof. U.N. Ghoshal[3] at considerable length, and a brief summary of his arguments would not be unreasonable here. Dr. Jayaswal's rendering of the phrase "*bhumer-adhipatir-hi saḥ*" of Manu as "The king is the protector of both the upper and sub-soil (*sic*,)" and his support from Medhātithi's commentary "that although no one knows what is there in the land and the government has to do very little guarding there, yet as there is a likelihood of the whole land being taken away by a strong enemy, the king is entitled to his share of this constructive protection" has been challenged on the grounds that "*bhumer-adhipatiḥ*" obviously does not mean the protector of the upper and the sub-soil and Medhātithi, while he states that the king is the protector of the land, in no way rejects his ultimate ownership of the soil.

Dr. Jayaswal's reading of a passage of Bhaṭṭasvāmin's[4]

1. *H.A.I.*, p, 164.
2. *Hindu Polity*, p. 330 ff.
3. *The Beginning of Indian Histoiography and Other Essays*, p. 158 ff.
4. Rāja., bhumeḥpatir-dṛṣṭah śāstrajñairudakasya Tābhyām-anyattu yaddravyaṃ tatra svāmyaṃ kuṭṭumbinām ll Quoted by U·N. Ghoshal in *The Beginning of Indian Historiography and other Essays*, p. 161. Jayaswal's rendering is very inaccurate in other particulars than that which we discuss; thus the last phrase should read "ownership is vested in householders not in family members."

commentary upon the *Arthaśāstra* as "The king is the protector, according to the opinion of the learned in the *śāstra* of the *bhūmi* (land) and water. Excepting these two whatever property there may be, his family members have sameness of right therein" has been corrected by Ghoshal in the light of the *Mānasollāsa* attributed to king Someśvara III of the western Cālukya dynasty, which observed that the king is declared to be the lord of all wealth, especially of that which is stored inside the earth; on the authority of Gaṇapati Śāstri Prof. Ghoshal has given the following translation of Bhaṭṭasvāmin's commentary : "The king is described by those who are learned in the *śāstras* as the lord of the soil and water : the householders have the same (right of property) in all things other than these two." Thus Prof. Ghoshal has found an unequivocal declaration of the king's right of property in the soil.

Finally, Ghoshal considers Dr. Jayaswal's study of a quotation from Mitramiśra's[1] *Rājanītiprakāśa,* which quotes the *Kātyāyana smṛti*[2], as follows : "When the king is called *svāmin* (master) of the land and in no case of any other wealth he only becomes entitled to receive the one-sixth share of the produce from it, not (that he is master) in any other way. The mastership which is connected with him is due to the habitation thereof by living beings and is the one-sixth share arising from their acts whether good or bad." On this passage the *Rājanītiprakāśa* comments "Its meaning is (this) : the king is called the *svāmin* of land, not of other wealth connected with land. Not in any other way is laid down as there is want of mastership in land. 'Living beings' are those having life; 'habitation thereof' is habitation of land; 'mastership', that is mastership of the king. Hence he can only receive one-sixth from their acts". Jayaswal's rendering of the passage has been challenged by Prof. Ghoshal on the following grounds—

(i) The word 'only' has nothing corresponding to it in the original text of Kātyāyana.

1. Asyārthaḥ l Rājā bhuvaḥ svāmī smṛtaḥ l Anyadravyasya bhūmisambaddhadravyasya an svāmī Anyathā bhūmisvāmyābhāve l Bhutānām Prāṇinām Tannivāsitvāt bhumivāsitvātl Svāmitvaṃ rājña iti Śeṣaḥ Ityataḥ tatkriyā baliṣaḍbhāgaṃ prāpnuyāt l Quoted by Ghoshal in *The Beginnings of Indian Historiography* p. 164.

2. Supra. p. 284, f.n. 1.

(ii) In Kātyāyana's verse above quoted *smṛtaḥ* is evidently taken by Dr. Jayaswal to be in the subjunctive and *prāpnuyāt* in the present tense. This is wrong and involves an unnecessary forcing of sense.

(iii) Dr. Jayaswal evidently understands *nānyathā in* Kātyāyana to stand for something like *nānyathā svāmiḥ smṛtaḥ*. But the natural connection of *nānyathā* is with *prāpnuyāt*. Besides how can *svāmi* be detached from the compound *bhūsavāmin* ?

(iv) If the word *anyathā bhūsvāmyabhāve* in the commentary were meant to be understood in Dr. Jayaswal's sense, Mitramiśra would have added a corresponding verb like *smṛtaḥ* to explain the meaning (cf. his explanation of the phrase '*tatkriyā*' in the same extract as *tatkriyābaliṣadbhāgam prāpnuyāt*) and *bhūmisvāmya* in would have had the fifth and not the seventh case ending. As it stands, it can only be taken to signify the commentator's sense that *nānyathā* means 'if the king were not owner of the land'.

Prof. Ghoshal's criticism appears to be fair enough and thus it would be unnecessary to give any more comment upon his statements. But Prof. Ghoshal seems later to have altered his opinion, and on his own part has elsewhere advanced a few obvious arguments to prove the existence of the private ownership of land.[1]

In his opening arguments Prof. Ghoshal has tried to establish the existence of the concept of full individual ownership both as regards movable and immovable property. He interprets, the word *svatva* as meaning ownership, but points out himself that ownership may be limited to the right of enjoyment, illustrating this with the statement of Manu that the field belongs to him who first removed the weed and the deer belongs to him who first wounded it.[2] The statement in question does not allow anybody the right of full ownership (*svatva*) but allows only the right of enjoyment, which Prof. Ghoshal himself admits. So it would not be unreasonable to agree with Dr. Derrett,[3] who, commenting upon the word *svatva*, holds that "In fact none of these related works (i.e.

1. *A.S.A.I.*, p. 84 ff
2. *Manu*, ix, 44.
3. *Bulletin of the S.O.A.S.*, 1956, p. 484.

mediaeval digests of Jīmūtavāhana, Raghunātha and others), deal with either the capacity to own, except very incidentally, or the incident of ownership, apart from the very general claim' to employ at pleasure''. Thus we see that other scholars as well as Prof. Ghoshal takes *svatva* to mean the right of enjoyment rather than outright ownership.

There-after Prof. Ghoshal has turned to the word *bhoga* and cites authority of Yājñavalkya, Bṛhaspati, Nārada and others in an attempt to show that it had the sense of ownership. But these passages have recently been reviewed by Dr. S.K. Maity[1], who has shown that they are survivals of a much earlier period, with little influence on contemporary practice. Thus, he writes, "it would appear that the earliest concept of the ownership of the land was derived from the first occupation, when there was less demand for land. But in later years, owing to the rapid advance of settled agricultural life, a more suitable form of ownership of the soil was demanded. Legal sanction was needed and hence the ancient jurists framed laws and regulations governing the ownership of land. These regulations duly safeguarded the interest of the possessor against a possible future challenge to the validity of the land of his possession. But to implement the laws absolute power was needed. And as a result of the growth of the royal power the king was more and more looked on as the absolute lord of the soil''.

The next argument of Prof. Ghoshal is based upon the statements of the *smṛtis* concerning different means of acquiring property. He cites passages of Manu, Nārada and Bṛhaspati, and tries to deduce that the means suggested by those authors are applicable to the land as well as to other forms of property. The quotation from Manu reads[2] "There are several lawful means of acquiring property—inheritance, finding, or friendly donations, purchase, conquest, lending at interest, the performance of work, and the acceptance of gifts

1. *The Economic Life of N.I. in the Gupta Period*. p. 25. ff.
2. Sapta vittāgamā dharmyā dāyo lābhaḥ krayo jayaḥ l
Prayogaḥ karmayogaśca satpratigraha eva ca ll 115 ll
Manu, ch. x.

from virtuous men." Nārada[1] gives six modes of getting property-finding, gift, purchase, valour, dowry, and inheritance from an issueless kinsman; while Bṛhaspati[2] states that immovable property may be acquired in seven different ways-by learning, by purchase, by mortgaging, by valour, with a wife, by inheritance, and by succession to the property of a kinsman who is issueless. These authors refer to the means of acquiring property in general and do not say anything specifically about land. Since they do not refer to land particularly, we cannot accept Prof. Ghoshal's assumption without question, as proof that the king had no claim to ultimate ownership of the land.

Quoting the authority of Manu, Prof. Ghoshal stated[3] that the compensation paid to the cultivator in cases of damage done to the crops suggests that the farmer was possessed of the land, which appears to be very inconclusive on the ground that such compensation might be expected even if the occupant had the mere right of enjoyment but no right of ownership. It is clear from many sources that farmers were expected to pay taxes to the king. In the absence of protection, which is the king's duty, the farmer can neither produce good crops nor pay the stipulated tax or rent to the royal treasury. Therefore, it was for the security of the farmer's crop that the compensation was paid to him in the event of damage done to the crop. Moreover the king's right to receive a fine for the damage done to the farmer's crop suggests that the king had the control over the land. Thus it appears that the king was the ultimate owner of the land.

Prof. Ghoshal[4] has referred to the authority of Kauṭilya, Gautama and others, who allowed the sale, gift and mortgage of land, which he took as an indication of the individual ownership of the land. But the text from Gautama[5] reads "Gold, a cow, a dress, a horse, land, sesamum, clarified

1. Labdhaṃ dānakrayaprāptaṃ śauryaṃ vaivāhikaṃ tathā l
Bāndhavāddāyasamprāptaṃ ṣaḍvidhastu dhanāgamaḥ ll Jājjā
Quoted by Ghoshal, p. 119.
2. *Br. Smrti*, ch. ix, v. 2.
3. *A.S.A.I.*, p. 87.
4. *A.S.A.I.*, pp 87 ff
5. *Gautama*, xix, 16.

butter and food are gifts which destroy sin." Here land has been mentioned as an object of gift but only in a general sense. Moreover the author does not say anything about the donor or the donee. The general rule may apply to the king or the privileged class, or to a donation made by individuals with the special permission of the king.

Prof. Ghoshal[1] has produced several examples of private donations to temples and the *Buddhist Saṁgha.* But we have to examine whether these donors were ordinary citizens or king's favourites. Prof. Ghoshal himself admits the latter in the cases of Jīvaka and Ambāpālī, who were a royal physician and the chief courtesan of an oligarchy or republic respectively in the time of the Buddha. When these people were attached to the royal service, they enjoyed special privileges, and the privileges enjoyed by the royal favourites cannot be accepted as an indication of the general conditions of the people. Therefore, it is unreasonable to accept the land donations of Jīvaka and others to the *Buddhist Saṁgha* as an indication of the private ownership of the land in India. Moreover, the conditions prevalent in Magadha at the time of Buddha throw very little light on our period, over a thousand years later. The example of the merchant Sudatta or Anāthapiṇḍaka, as quoted by Prof. Ghoshal, gives quite a different impression. It suggests that though Sudatta was a man of fortune, he had no land whatever to donate. But his intense desire to earn righteousness by donating land to the Buddhist Saṁgha made him apply to the Buddhist prince Jeta for the transfer of some land which he could give to the Buddhist Saṅgha. There are few epigraphic records to this effect. A copper plate grant of Dharmāditya records that Vātabhoga[2] applied for permission to buy some land to donate. The grant of the time of Gopacandra[3] records the request of the donor in the following terms : "With respectful mind, thus (I would wish) through your honour's favour to buy at the proper price about so much cultivated land as can be sown with a *kulya* of seed", which shows that donors had to get

1. *A.S.A.I.*, p. 89.
2. *I.A.*, vol. 39, p. 195.
3. *Ibid.*, p. 204.

special permission to buy land for donation. Thus the existence of land specially bought for donation cannot be adopted as an example of private ownership. The cases cited by Prof. Ghoshal show that usufructuary possession (*bhoga*) of land was often vested in individuals or religious bodies. But the numerous inscriptions and other evidence, which show that such land could only be given away or otherwise transferred with official permission, surely indicate that the king was the owner of the land.

Prof. Ghoshal's reference to the Gwalior[1] inscription of the year 933 and to the Siyadoni inscription, is again a misrepresentation of the actual facts. The inscription states that the whole town (Samasthāna) gave to a temple a piece of land in the village of Cūḍapallikā, which was the town's own property[2] (*svabhujyam*). The inscription in question shows that the land belonged to the town and not to a private person and it was the townsmen who donated the land. Thus we have here reference of the communal ownership of the land, which we shall consider later, certainly not to its individual ownership. The inscription moreover refers to the land as being merely in the possession (*bhujya*) of the town and in no way excludes the possibility of the king's ultimate ownership of and authority over it. Prof. Ghoshal's reference to the Siyādoni inscription is similar in purport and open to the same objection.

Prof. Ghoshal has tried to make distinction between the private land and the crown land on the authority of the *Kauṭilya Arthasāstra*[3]. He refers to a passage in the text which reads: "Fields that are left unsown may be brought under cultivation by employing those who cultivate for half the share in the produce or those who live by their own physical exertion cultivate such fields for 1/4 or 1/5 of the produce

---

1. *A.S.A.I.*, pp. 90 ff.
2. *E.I.*, vol. i, p. 159, lines 3-5.
3. Vāpātiriktamardhasītikāḥ kuryuḥ l
Svavīryopajīvinovā caturthapañcabhāgikāḥ
yatheṣṭamanavasitaṃ bhagaṃ dadyuranyatra
kṛcchrebhyaḥ svasetubhyaḥ ll
K. Arthaśāstra, Book, ii, ch. 24. p. 116.

grown or they may pay an unspecified proportion as decided upon". Prof. Ghoshal has accepted Shamasastry's translation. In fact nothing is said about the private land. The word *setu* is not attested in this sense and must mean an embankment. We suggest that the difficult phrase *anyatra kṛcchrebhyaḥ svasetubhyas* implies "except when they themselves have embanked the land in question with much labour" before cultivating it; such a tenant should be allowed a large share of crops. Hence Shamasastry's "as much as they can without entailing any hardship upon themselves" is an unjustified translation.

Elsewhere Kauṭilya[1] stated that "the king who is desirous of getting back the land leased for settlement to another, when the latter has lost his men and money in cultivating it, should first make an agreement with such a purchaser as is weak, base-born, devoid of energy, helpless, of unrighteous character, addicted to evil ways, trusting to fate and indiscreet in his actions. When the cultivation of the land entails much expenditure of men and money and when a weak base-born man attempts to colonize it, he will perish along with his people in consequence of his loss of men and money. Though strong, a base-born man will be deserted by his people, who do not like him lest they may come to grief under him, though possessing an army he cannot employ it if he is devoid of energy, and such an army will perish in consequence of the loss incurred by its master; though possessing wealth, a man who hesitates to part with his money and shows favour to none cannot find help in any quarter; and when it is easy to drive out a man of unrighteous character from the land in which he has firmly established himself none can expect that man of unrighteous character would be capable of cultivating a tract of wasteland and keeping it secure. The same fact explains the fate of such a tenant as is addicted to evil ways: whoever, trusting to fate and putting no reliance on manliness, withdraws himself from energetic work, will perish without undertaking anything or without achieving anything from his undertaking; and whoever is indiscreet in his actions will achieve nothing and is the worst (of tenants), "Thus we find several ways

1. *K. Arthaśāstra*, Book, vii, ch. xi, p. 297 (text) p. 324. (Fifth Edition - English translation).

and means advocated by Kauṭilya to dispossess those tenants from the field once given them to cultivate. If these tenants had any proprietory right over the land Kauṭilya would scarcely have advised the king to do so.

Prof. Ghoshal[1] has strengthened his arguments by his interpretation of the terms *bhāgabhogakara*, *udraṅga*, aud *uparikara* occurring to many inscriptions. In his opinion *udraṅga* and *uparikara* stand for the revenue coming from crown land, while *bhāgabhogakara*, *hiraṇya* and other terms were used for the revenue coming from the land possessed by individuals. But an analysis of the occurrence of these revenue terms suggests that they were different regional usages, because inscriptions fron western India such as the Rājor inscription of Mathanadeva[2], the Sarsvani plates of Biddharāja, two grants of Dhurvasena etc. contain the words *udraṇga* and *uparikara*, while the Banskhera[3] and Madhuban plates of Harṣa, and the Vanagoan plates of the Pāla king Madanapāla contain the word *bhāgabhogakara* for royal revenue. Thus we find different terms occurred for the same tax in different geographical regions. Therefore on such a vague basis it appears difficult to accept a theory that affects a vital point of ancient Indian history.

On the authority of Ṇārada[4], Prof. Ghoshal admits that rulers were entitled to dispossess their tenants, but claims that this right did not depend on the royal ownership of land but on the king's sovereign rights. The reference in question reads "A field which has been held by three generations in succession and a house which has been inherited from another cannot be estranged (from their legal owners) by force of possession except when the king wills it." Here thc author refers to disputed land, which has little bearing on the subject. Moreover the passage in question is a suggestion for the decision of

1. *Hindu Revenue System*. pp. 29. ff.
2. *E.I.*, vol, iii, p. 266.
   E.I., vol. vi, p. 298.
   E.I., vol. viii, p. 199.
3. *E.I.*, vol. xxxx, part II, p. 56, line 34.
   E.I., vol. i, p. 73, *E.I.*, vol. iv. p. 211.
4. *A.S.A.I.* p. 96.

court cases and does not imply the full hereditary rights of the occupants. Furthermore, It declares that the king at will can override claims based on long-standing occupancy. In fact it would seem that the author looks on the king as the ultimate owner of the land and the text must be interpreted in an almost opposite sense to the interpretation of Prof. Ghoshal.

Prof. Ghoshal[1] holds that Bṛhaspati denies the king the right of arbitrary transfer of village holdings, and his hypothesis is based upon the verse: "When land is taken from one person by a king actuated by anger or avarice or using a fraudulent pretext and bestowed on a different person as a mark of his favour, such a gift is not considered as valid"[2]. The passage in question concerns the resumptions of a gift. It was not expected that the king should resume donated lands, but if he did so out of anger or avarice the people were advised to disobey his command on such an occasion. But such occasions were no doubt very rare and we are not concerned with them in the present work. However, the resumption of land by the king suggests his ultimate ownership.

Prof. Ghoshal[3] appears to be somewhat confused in his interpretation of Medhātithi's commentary on Manu. He translates the relevant passage as "The king should get a share of that which is produced from the land belonging to him". Prof. Ghoshal took the word *tadiyāyāḥ bhuvo* as implying the royal land in a special sense. But Medhātithi's statement in its full context means something quite different. The passage specially refers to treasure-trove and not to crops: "Though when the treasure is buried, there is no need for any royal protection, yet it is open to the risk of being taken away by some powerful person; so that there is need for the king's care. It is with a view to this that it has been said he is the lord of the soil. He is the lord (*prabhu*) of the soil and when something

1. *A.S.A.I.*, p. 95.
2. *Bṛhaspati*, xix, 22.
3. Yadyapi kṣitau nihitasya kenacidajñānānna rājakīyarakṣopayujyate tathāpi tasya balavatāpahāraḥ sambhāvyate l Ato'styevarakṣāyā arthavattvam l Etadarthamevāha bhūmeradhipatirhisaḥ l Prabhurasau bhumestadīyāyāśca bhuvo yallabdhaṃ tatra yuktaṃ tasya bhāgādānam l
Medhātithi on Manu, viii, 39.

has been obtained out of the soil, that belongs to him, it is only right that he should receive his share of it". It is well-known that the king had rights over all treasure-trove in the kingdom. Thus we see that the term '*tadiyāyābhuvo*' stands for the king's whole territory and not for the royal land as contended by Prof. Ghoshal. In fact the text he quotes is completely opposed to the doctrine of private ownership.

A second point regarding which Prof. Ghoshal is confused is the interpretation of word *taṣya bhāgadānam*. According to Prof. Ghoshal it stands for the king's share of the land produce. But Medhātithi[1] used the word in a different sense. He stated : "There are treasure-troves that have lain under the ground for hundreds or even a thousand years. If when the ground is being dug, such a treasure-trove is somehow found by someone, it belongs to the king. As says Gautama[2] : 'Treasure-trove when found is the king's property. But this applies only to the case of a treasure, the original hoarder of which is not known. And with regard to this it has been laid down that one who reports the find is to receive one-sixth of it. If a man says "this is mine" 'truly', i.e. on reliable evidence from him, the king shall take the sixth part at which the king's share has been fixed. That is the king is to take the sixth part of that treasure-trove of which the rightful owner has been discovered with certainty. This option regarding the 'sixth or the twelfth part' is based upon the qualities of the finder. The rule here laid down applies to the case where the treasure belongs to the brāhmaṇas; when however its rightful owner is not known then, even though it may have been found by a learned brāhmaṇa, the king's share has to be paid, as it is going to be declared (in verse 39) "that of all ancient hoards the king is entitled to one-sixth". Thus it is clear that the phrase '*tasya bhāgadānam*' of Medhātithi here stands for the king's share in the treasure-trove and not in the produce of the land as interpreted by Prof. Ghoshal.

A third objection raised by Prof. Ghoshal[3] against the

---

1. *Medhātithi on Manu.*, viii, 35-37.
2. *Gautama*, x, 43.
3. *A.S.A.I.*, p. 99.

interpretation of Manu's statement as implying royal ownership of the land is : "In the text of Manu declaring the king to be the lord of the soil, he is constrained to refer to the traditional view of the taxes being the king's fee for protection as an additional argument for supporting his case while he advances on behalf of the brāhmaṇas in the same context the still more sweeping claim to be the "owners of everything' a claim which indeed goes back to the period of the later *saṃhitās*." In other words Manu makes a sweeping and exaggerated statement, not to be taken seriously, in order to prove the king's right over the treasure-trove. But it is not only Manu who declared that the king was entitled to a share of the find, but Gautama[1] and others also declared that the king was entitled to a share. So if Manu had to emphasise his case, he might have quoted the earlier authorities or otherwise expanded his verse, instead of stating that the king was the lord of the soil if it had been generally accepted that he was not, Moreover if Manu's remark had been a sweeping statement and not intended to be taken literally, Medhātithi would scarcely have given it so much attention. Thus he did not claim that brāhmaṇas are the lords of all, because he knew that it was not true in practice. So if Manu's statement had been merely rhetorical Medhātithi would not have taken trouble to state that the king is the master of the soil, and that, as it belongs to him, it is only right that he should receive his share of its produce.

Commenting upon the verse of Kātyāyana[2] in an answer to Dr. Barnett's[3] criticism Prof. Ghoshal[4] stated : "The express statements of Kātyāyana and other authorities are not connected with any specific rights of ownership belonging to the king but are used (as I indicated in my Agrarian System) solely to explain or justify the king's right to levy certain revenue from land." In other words Kātyāyana's statement is a pretext to justify the king's right to levy taxes

1. *Gautama Smṛti*, x, 47.
2. *Infra*
3. *J.R.A.S.*, 1931, p. 694.
4. *I.H.Q.*, vol. vii, p. 659.

from the land. But had the verse been a mere pretext, it would certainly have been worded differently, and given stronger emphasis. On the other hand the text specifically states that king is the owner of the land, as we shall see later.

Prof. Ghoshal's further reply[1] to Dr. Barnett's comment regarding the evidence of the foreign accounts is that "Dr. Barnett is extremely unfair to me because he stated that 'Ghoshal has explained away Megasthenes by a not very probable supposition'." Prof. Ghoshal's original statement on these accounts was : "They have not obtained much credence even from those who believe in the state ownership of soil in ancient India, while the testimony of the Chinese pilgrims is only implicit in its chararacter"[2], which in fact is no comment at all. We have the interpretation of B.C.J. Timmer, who after examining the statements of various Greek and Latin sources, and comparing them with the Indian, held that all land was ultimately owned by the king.[3] Breloer[4], after careful consideration of the foreign and literary sources, also stated that the whole land belonged to the king. And there is no reason to doubt that these authors do not believe in their own statements. Turning to the third objection raised by Dr. Barnett that "the cases where kings actually resumed grants of land made to brāhmaṇas, or reserve to themselves the right to do so in the event of misconduct" suggest that the king was the owner of the land, Prof. Ghoshal stated : "It is difficult to understand the relevancy of Dr. Barnett's argument. Cases of actual or potential resumption of endowments of lands made by the kings in favour of brāhmaṇas, as Dr. Barnett well knows, are altogether exceptional in character. But even if they were very much more numerous the condition of their tenure would apply only to the fiscal or other rights emanating from the crown".[5] This is perhaps true in some cases of religious donations where the donees had only the fiscal rights over the land. But it throws little light on the

1. *I.H.Q.*, vol. vii, p. 659.
2. *A.S.I.A.*, pp. 98-99.
3. *Megasthenes on de Indische Maatachappij*, p. 123.
4. *Kauṭalīya-Studien*, vol. i, p. 53.
5. *I.H.Q.*, vol. vii, p. 660.

question of whether or not the land ultimately belonged to the king. That a king should grant the taxes of a given area to a religious cause may be taken to suggest rather that he was ultimate owner of that area than the reverse. Moreover, many land grants give further rights and it is clear that often the donees settled on the land and tilled it by hired labourers.[1]

Prof. Ghoshal's further examples, showing the private ownership of land in modern India, have nothing to do with the problem in our period. So we may appropriately conclude our comments on Dr. Ghoshal's theories here.

Recently Dr. Lallan ji Gopal[2] has tried to prove the individual ownership of land on the basis of Medhātithi's comment on Manu II vv. 246. Possibly Dr. Gopal has not studied the verse in its proper context. The verse under question is a piece of advice to the sovereign and the sovereign has been advised to donate arable land or land suitable for making building to the teacher as *guru dakṣinā*. Thus the nature of this donation is absolutely different from others. Secondly, such verses do not limit the ultimate ownership of the king. Lastly, we have a number of examples where we find the sovereign dispossessing the legal owners[3] which make us think that the owners had only usurpractary rights while the ultimate ownership laid with the king.

Prof. Altekar[4] is another authority who, on the evidence of Nārada and a few other sources, has tried to prove that the private ownership of land existed in ancient India. His reference to Nārada reads[5] that houses and land were the homes of householders, and therefore the king should not confiscate them. It refers to plots of land meant for building purposes and says next to nothing regarding the ownership of land under cultivation It says next to nothing about the ownership of the land.

A second objection raised by Prof. Altekar[6] is that the

1. *E. I.*, vol. i, p. 283, *E.I.*, vol. ii, p. 179.
2. The Economic life in Northern India, f. 4.
3. Infra pp. 142, 144, 145.
4. *S.G.A.I.*, p. 200.
5. *Nārada*, ni. 42.
6. *S.G.A.I.*, p. 202.

king, if he had been owner of the whole land, would not have donated land in fragments on certain occasions. For example Dhruvasena I of Valabhi donated 360 *pādāvartas* of land in several pieces. This objection of Prof. Altekar appears to be fallacious, because we have to take into consideration that rulers of the period used to make donations several times during their lifetimes. If once a certain piece of land was donated, the donee was not to be dispossessed from that land, otherwise it was believed that the king would commit a heinous sin; this is stated many times in our epigraphic records.[1] Bearing this point in mind we can argue that the king did not dare to dispossess the earlier occupants, so he donated the land in several plots.

The third objection raised by Prof. Altekar[2] is that if the king had been the owner of the land the Emperor Amoghavarṣa of the Deccan would not have donated the village of Taleyur and a flower garden in the same village separately, and Govindacandra of Kanauj would not have donated the village Lollisapāda together with the Tivāyi-kṣetra, also believed by Altekar to be in the same village, in the district of Umrāla. The example of Amoghavarṣa quoted by Prof. Altekar does not concern us immediately because it applies to the Deccan. However, the inscription[3] refers to a donation of the village of Taleyur and a flower-garden 500x150 cubits in dimension, situated in the same village. The relevant phrase of the inscription reads : "*dvādaśa puṣpavāṭaḥ paṃcāśad-uttaraśata-hasta-vistāraḥ paṁcaśata-hasta-pramāṇ-āyāmaḥ*. These compounds are in apposition to the name of the village and follow the list of the taxes to which the temple is entitled. There are evidently twelve small flower gardens involved and not one, as Prof. Alteker states. It is by no means clear that the temple was given unlimited power over them, and in view of their mention together with the taxes it may well be that the passage merely implies that the temple had rights over the flowers grown there.

---

1. *E.I.*, vol. i, p. 88, etc.
2. *S.G.A.I.*, p. 202 ff.
3. *E.I.* vol. vi, p. 32, lines 40-41.

Govindacandra's inscription[1], to which Prof. Altekar specially refers, makes no reference to a separate field. In it Govindacandra addresses "The dwellers in the village of Lollisapāda together with Tivāyikṣetra in the district of Umrāla." Apparently Tivāyi-kṣetra is Prof. Altekar's field. But in the description of the gift this is not separately mentioned, and it appears that the king merely donated the village with the normal rights over it to a brāhmaṇa Dāmodaraśarman. It seems quite clear that Tivāyi-kṣetra is some outlying settlement attached to the village for revenue purpose, and not a field within the village.

Both Dr. Jayaswal[2] and Prof. Ghoshal[3] have quoted the authority of Jaimini's *Mīmāṁsāsūtra* and several commentators upon it, to suggest that the individual ownership of land existed in ancient India. The text states that the landed property cannot be given as fee for the Viśvajit sacrifice because it is not the special property of anyone. This statement of Jaimini certainly refutes the royal ownership of land, but it also appears to contradict the individual ownership of land. Thus when the author says[4] that the land does not belong to anyone, it implies either that the land belonged to the community or was absolutely free of all ownership whatsoever. The passage has been clarified by Mādhavācārya[5] who devided the land under two heads—*Mahābhūmi* and; Asādhāraṇa. His commentary runs as follows : "(It may be said that) When a *Sārvabhauma* king gives away everything in a *viśvajit* or similar (sacrifice) the whole land (*mahābhūmi*), together with pasture, high roads, and waters, is to be given by him. Why ? Because the earth is his property (*dhanatva*).

---

1. The reference given by Prof. Altekar is incidentally wrong, but it is clear that the inscription to which he refers is to be found in *E.I.*, vol. viii, p. 159.

2. *Hindu Polity*. p. 331 ff.

3. *A.S.A.I.*, p. 99 ff.

4. Na bhūmiḥ syātsarvānpratyaviśiṣṭatvāt 77. 3. ll

5. Yadā sārvabhaumo rājā viśvajidādau sarvasvaṃ dadāti l Tadā gopathamārgajalāśayādyanvitā mahābhūmistena dātavyā l Kutaḥ l Bhumestadīyadhanatvāt l Rājā sarvasyeṣṭe brāhmaṇavarjamiti smṛteriti prāpte brūmaḥ ll Duṣṭaśikṣāśiṣṭaparipālanābhyāṃ rājña īśitṛtvaṃ smṛtyabhipretamiti na rājño bhūmirdhanam l Kiṃtu tasyāṃ tasyāṃ bhumau svakarmaphalabhūnjānānāṃ sarveṣāṃ prāṇināṃ sādhāraṇaṃ dhanam l Ato'sādhāraṇasya bhūkhaṇḍasya satyapi dāne mahābhumer dānaṃ nāsti ll
Jaimīnīya-Nyāyamālā-Vistāra, Ch. 6, sec. 7, v. 3, p. 291.

The king rules all things except brāhmaṇa according to the *smṛtis*. If this be accepted we declare : the rulership of the king is intended for the correction of evil doers and the protection of the cultured, in the view of the *Smṛtis*. The earth is not the property (*dhana*) of the king but the common property (*sādharaṇaṃ dhanam*) of all beings who enjoy the result of their past deeds. Hence, though there may be the gift of a piece of land not held in common, (*asādhāraṇa*) there can be no gift of the whole land (*mahābhūmi*)". In this text we see that the king's right over the common land has not been recognized, but is admitted over certain land. The word *sādhāraṇa* has been taken by Prof. Ghoshal to mean individual ownership, but the word in fact stands for belonging to all, general, common, universal etc.[1] Thus we find Mādhavācārya maintaining the communal ownership of the land.

Commenting upon the same sūtra of Jaimini, Śabarasvāmī stated[2] : "The earth cannot be given away; people are found to be the owners (*īśitāraḥ*) of fields, not of the entire terrestrial globe. Says the opponent : 'One who happens to be the lord of the whole earth (*sārvabhauma*) may give it away'.

"'Even he cannot give it away', we reply.—'Why ?' 'Because the enjoyment that the lord of the earth derived from the control of the earth (*yāvatā bhogena sārvabhaumo bhumer īṣṭe*) is precisely like that which another man has. From his protection of corn and other crops (produced from the earth) has authority over (*īṣṭe*) a certain share which he has earned but not the earth itself. When the support and progress etc. of all beings is caused by the earth and not by the men who are settled upon it there is no distinction in its lordship. Therefore the earth is not to be given'." Here we find the

1. *Sanskrit English Dictionary* by Sir M.M. Williams, p. 2A2.

2. Na bhūmirdeyā iti l Kutaḥ l Kṣetrāṇāmīśitāro manuṣyā dṛśyante, na kṛtsnasya pṛthvīgolakasyeti ll Āha l Ya idānim sārvabhaumaḥ sa tarhi dāsyati l So'pi neti brūmaḥ l Kutaḥ l Yāvatā bhogena sārvabhaumo bhūmerīṣṭe, tāvata nyo'pi, Na tatra kaścidviśeṣaḥ l Sārvabhaumatvesya tvetadadhikam, yadasau pṛthivyāṃ sambhūtānāṃ vrīhyādīnāṃ rakṣaṇena nirviṣṭasya kasyacid bhāgasya īṣṭe, na bhumeḥ l Tannirviṣṭāśca ye manuṣyāstairanyat sarvaprāṇināṃ dhāraṇavikramaṇādi yad bhūmikṛtam, tatreśitvaṃ prati na kaścidviśeṣaḥ l Tasmānna bhūmirdeyā ll *Mīmāṃsādarśana*, ch. 6 sec. 7 v. 3.

commentator stating that the king has the same right of enjoyment of land as others have. He indicates the others in the plural. If the author had had the individual ownership of land in his mind he would have referred to the matter in the singular number, rather than in the plural. Secondly, when Śabarasvāmi specifically mentioned that the king's authority over land was not stronger than common people and the rent paid to him was part of remuneration for the protection he offered to the land or crops. Thus the occurrence of the phrase *Yāvatā bhogena sārvabhaumo bhumer īṣṭe* refer to the communal ownership and not the king's ownership of land.

Khaṇḍadeva refuted the royal ownership of land in a most authoritative manner, but said nothing about its ownership by the individual. He stated:[1] "Even the *sārvabhauma* cannot have the ownership (*svatva*) of it (the Earth), because even conquest produces proprietary rights (*svatva*) only with regard to the wealth, houses, fields etc. owned by the enemy, while as far as the whole land (*mahā-pṛthvī*) is concerned sovereignty (*rājyam*) arises from the creation of authority (*adhikāra*) through conquest. Now sovereignty consists only in protecting one's kingdom and rooting out the thorns, and for this reason taxes are taken from peasants and fines from offenders, but no proprietory right (*svatva*) in it (the Earth) arises therefrom. If it were so he would claim ownership over the leaves and wood in the forests. There would arise obstruction to the practice of getting and selling property and it would happen that the people and houses in his kingdom were his own property. Therefore it is not to be given." Here we have no example of either the royal ownership or the individual ownership of land. Ownership of houses and trees cannot be taken as precedents for the ownership of land. Hence the passage

1. Sārvabhaumasyāpi na tasyām svatvam l Jayasyāpi śatrusvāmikadhanagṛhakṣetrādiviṣaya eva svatvotpādakatvāt l Mahāpṛthivyāṃ tu rājyamātrādhikārasyaiva jayenasampādanāt l Rājyaṃ hi svaviṣaya paripālanaṃkaṇṭakoddharaṇarūpam l Tannimittakaṃ ca tasya karṣakebhyaḥ karādānaṃ daṇḍyebhyaśca daṇḍādānmityetāvanmātram l Na tvetāvatā tasyāṃ svatvam l Tathātve vanagatatṛṇakāṣṭhādāvapi svatvāpattau tatra svatvotpādakaparikrayavidhivirodhāpatteḥ l Tadviṣayasthaprajāgṛhādiṣvapi svatvāpatteśca l Tasmānnāsau deyā l Bhaṭṭadīpikā, ch. 6, sec. 7, v. 3, p. 493.

implies that ultimately the community was possessed of the land.

Commenting upon Manu[1], Medhātithi refuted the individual ownership of land in the following words : "Who can be owner (*svāmi*) of all this extensive earth ? Who too can take it away by force ? For there is no king over the whole earth (*sārvabhauma*). To this effect there is the song of the earth addressed to Viśvakarman Bhauvana, the latter term being his name derived from his father : 'No mortals can give me away"; which means there is no one who owns the entire earth;—'I shall sink into the midst of the water, having heard that he is desirous of having intercourse with me:—this sinking within water implying the futility of the gift. 'Vain is thy promise to give me away:—just as what is thrown in water becomes useless......The earth is the common property of all men (*sarvasādhāraṇa*) to be equally enjoyed by all, and kings have a share in it only through their office of protection *rakṣānirbandhamātra*)."

Thus according to the statement of Medhātithi the king is only the protector of the land and not the owner. The author continues that no mortal has possessed land. This suggests that no individual has hereditary rights over the land. The commentator is then faced with the problem as to who is the owner of the field, and gives the answer that land is common property.

Examples of communal ownership of land are not very frequent in Northern India. Both Prof. Altekar[2] and Dr. Basak[3] have referred to the "A copper plate of Dharmāditya

1. Nanviyatyāḥ kaḥ svāmi ko vā'pahartā l Na hi sārvabhaumaḥ kaścidasti l Tathā ca gāthā bhūmeḥ—na māṃ martyaḥ kaścana dātumarhati l Na kaścitsārvabhaumo'stītyabhiprāyaḥ l Viśvakarman dāsitha bhauvanamādiviśvakarmabhaumneti piṭṛv yapàdeśena svanāmnā ca rājñāmantraṇam śrutam mayā'sau rantumicchatīti upamaisyati salilasya madhye nimajje'haṃ salilasya madhyamevaṃ saṃkalpaṃ vṛthā saṃkalpitavati tvayi salile majjāmi l Salilamajjanena naiṣphalyamatra dānasaṃkalpasyāḥ l Yathā salile nikṣiptaṃ niṣphalemevametadapīti l Mṛṣaiṣa Kaśyapāya saṃgaraḥ l Tavaiṣa saṃgaraḥ pratiśravaḥ pretijñānaṃ Kaśyapāya dadāmīti mogho vandhyo'stu sarvasādhāraṇā'ham l Sarvajanopabhogyā l Kevalaṃ rājāno rakṣānirbandhamātrabhāja ityabhiprāyaḥ l

Medhātithi *on Manu*, viii, 99. Parts of the passage are evidently corrupt, Our translation is based on that of Ganganath Jha.

2. *The Vākātaka-Gupta Age*, p. 333.

3. *Āshutosh Mukherjee Silver Jubilee*, vol. iii, part ii, p. 487., *I.A.*, vol. p. 195 ff.

of East Bengal. The inscription reads that the village assembly, headed by seventeen members who are mentioned by name, were apprised by Vātabhoga, thus :—'I wish to buy a piece of cultivated land from your honours and to bestow it on a brāhmaṇa, therefore do you deign to take the price from me to divide the land in the *viṣaya* and to give it to me.' Here we find no trace of individual ownership. The donor Vātabhoga has to buy land from the village council who were responsible for the administration of the village land. Thus the right of the land administration was vested in the village assembly, which implies the communal ownership of the land. There are several references to this effect in the South India epigraphic records, to one of which Prof. Majumdar[1] has referred. A certain brāhmaṇa who could not pay the revenue returned the land to the village assembly and left the village during the reign of Kullotunga I[2], the Cola king. In the 45th year of the same king's reign a similar incident took place, and the land was confiscated by the village assembly of Konirirājapuram. Thus the communal ownership of land is to be found both in theory and practice. But what this communal ownership of land amounted to is a matter of further investigation. Prof. Basak,[3] basing his view on the inscription of Dharmāditya to which we have referred above, held that "it seems clear that one-sixth of the price of the sold land went to the king, perhaps because he was the protector of the realm, and that the remaining five sixths went to swell the local funds of the village assembly". Prof. Basak has produced only one piece of evidence to suggest that the village assembly held five-sixths of the price of the land. The phrase in question reads *Paramabhaṭṭāraka-pādānām attra dharmmaṣaḍbhāgalābhaḥ*[4] and Prof. Basak's interpretation appears to be a forced reading. As Dr. D.C. Sircar[5] has conclusively shown, the *dharma-ṣaḍbhāga* referred to is not to be taken as the sixth part of the selling price due to the

1. *Corporate Life in Ancient India*, p. 186.
2. *South Indian Epigraphic Report*, 1910, p. 92.
3. *I.A.*, 1910, p. 195. ff. line 13.
4. *I.A.*, 1910, p. 195 ff. line 13.
5. *S. Sanskrit Inscriptions*, p. 332, note 5.

king, but the sixth part of the religious merit of the gift, which was thought to compensate the king for the loss of revenue involved in the donation of the land to religious causes. Thus even the one example produced by Prof. Basak appears to be faulty. On the other hand, South Indian Inscriptions show that in the time of Rajendra I Coladeva, the whole tax collected by the village assembly went to the royal treasury[1]. Thus it would not be unreasonable to conclude with Dr. R. C. Majumdar[2] that "the village assembly were *practically* (our italics) the absolute proprietor of the village land, including fresh clearings, and were responsible for the total amount of revenue to the king."

If once we accept that the village assemply was responsible for the payment of the total amount of the revenue to the king, then it appears as an intermediary between the king and the people. The copper plate grant to the time of Dharmāditya, to which we have already referred, suggests that the village elders were working in accordance with the will of the king. Inscriptions of reign of Kullotuṅga, as seen above, suggest that the village head-man carried out the command of the king and confiscated the property of those who failed to pay the royal taxation in the name of the king, which is against the very spirit of communal ownership. Thus the village assembly as the community of land-owners appears to royal agent of land management, responsible rather to the king than to the people. Thus the king through these local bodies controlled the whole land of his kingdom.

Even in the passage quoted from different *Mimāṃsā* commentators we find evidence of a school which all the time favoured the royal ownership of land.

Nārada[3] stated that on failure of the daughter the near relatives (*sakulya*) are to succeed, and after them the remoter relatives (*bāndhava*), next members of the same clan (*sajāti*), but that in default of all heirs wealth should go to the king. Bṛhaspati[4] stated that in case of kṣatriyas, vaiśyas and śūdras

1. *South Indian Epigraphic Report*, 1915, p. 98.
2. *Corporate Life in Ancient India*, p. 186.
3. *Nārada*, niii, 51.
4. Ye' putrāḥ kṣatraviṭcchūdrāḥ patnībhrātṛvivarjitāḥ l
   Teṣām dhanaharo rājā sarvasyādhipatirhi saḥ ll
   Brhas., p. 216, v. 119.

who die without leaving descendents, brothers or wife, their property should go to the king because he is the lord of all things, presumably including land. Kullūka Bhaṭṭa[1], commenting upon Manu, stated that the property of the three classes in the absence of any descendant should go to the king. Medhātithi[2] expressed the same view. Thus we see that the king claimed the property of the man who died without any heir, and Bṛhaspati justified his demand on the ground that he was the master of the whole earth. Had the ultimate ownership of the land been vested in the village community those lawgivers would have authorised it to take over the land of the dead man. Thus the king's recovery of the man's property suggests that the king was regarded as ultimate owner of the land.

Authors of the period have referred to different rates of taxation. For example, Lakṣmīdhara[3] laid it down as one-sixth, one-eighth or one-twelfth; Kātyāyana[4] stated it as one-sixth only, while Śukra[5] demanded one-third, one-fourth, or even one half of the land produce. Thus the different rates of taxation show that there was no fixed revenue and that the amount paid varied according to the crop. Had there been individual ownership of land there would have been something like the permanent settlement of modern days and a fixed rate of revenue. The levying of taxes in this manner suggests that the king had still a direct interest in the produce of the soil, and that the peasant was looked on as in some sense his tenant or agent, a sharecropper with an unusually large share of the produce. Thus the whole land-revenue system seems to presuppose royal ownership of land.

Referring to the two contradictory passages in Medhātithi Ghoshal holds[6] "These principles relate, successively to the king's ownership of the soil entitling him to his share of its underground wealth and to the title of the first clearer to the

---

1. Kṣatriyādi-dhanaṃ punaḥ purvokta-rikthaharābhāve rājāgṛhṇīyāt l *Kullūka on Manu*, ix, 189.
2. *Medhātithi on Manu*, ix. 189.
3. *Kṛtya Kalpa.*, p. 90.
4. *Kāt.*, v. 1*v*.
5. *Śukra*, ch. iv. sec. ii, *v*. 227-230.
6. *A History of Indian Political Ideas*, *p*. 426.

soil and its products". The two extracts from Medhātithi, which are elsewhere considered[1], appear to be contradictory. One refers to the royal ownership while the other seems to maintain the communal ownership of land. But if the communal ownership of land had been in Medhātithi's mind, he would surely have stated the fact more clearly. The passage in which Medhātithi seems to support the communal ownership of land must be read in its context, with the famous brāhmaṇic story of Viśvakarman Bhauvana. The specific statement of the Earth Goddess that she was common property and not to be given away could not be explicity rejected by any brāhmaṇa commentator, since it occurred in a text of great sanctity.[2] But it is clear that the story arose at a time when kings had only just begun to claim powers over the land, and this story must represent a protest on the part of some thinkers against this tendency. It had little practical validity over a thousand years later, in the times we are considering, and we must look on Medhātithi's apparent support of communal ownership, like that of the Mimāṃsā commentators to whom we have referred above, as pious theorising. In practice, as we see from his treatment of the question of treasure-trove, Medhātithi admitted the king's ownership of the land, because he admitted that the king is the owner of the soil. This statement of Medhātithi is corroborated by another important commentator of Manu, Kullūkabhaṭṭa[3], who also maintained that the king is the ultimate owner of the land and so should get the proper share of the land produce. Thus the statements of Manu stood in favour of the royal ownership of land in our period.

Kātyāyana[4] very emphatically stated that the king is the owner of the soil, and for that reason is entitled to one-sixth of the land produce. Since living beings inhabit the land therefore they pay the agricultural tax. This implies that the king

1. Supra, p.
2. *Ait.* Br., ch. iv. sec. viii, 21, p. 336.
3. *Kullūkabhaṭṭa on Manu*, viii, 39.
4. Bhūsvāmī tu smṛto rājā nānyadravyasya sarvadā l
Tatphalasya hi saḍbhāgaṃ prāpnuyānnānyathaivatu ll
Bhūtānāṃ tannivāsitvātsvāmitvaṃ tena kīrtitam l
Tat kriyā bali-ṣaḍbhāgaṃśubhāśubhanimittajam ll
Kāt., 16-17.

was the absolute owner of the land and it was by virtue of ownership that he received the revenue. People residing on the earth were his subjects and made their livelihood out of his land; therefore they were liable to pay the *bali* to the royal treasury.

Bṛhaspati[1] stated that the land abandoned by rivers or granted by the king belongs to him who receives it. Otherwise there would be no acquisition through fate or the king among men. Loss and gain and life among men depend on the act of fate and of the king; therefore, in all affairs what is affected by them must not be rescinded. This implies that the possession of the land can be valid only when the king approves it and nobody can have land without his approval. Bṛhaspati did not stop here but continued that "when land is taken from a person enjoying it without a legitimate title of ownership and given to a worthier person (the latter) must not be deprived of it." This implies that the king was possessed of the power to dispossess tenants as he liked, which again suggests that the king was the owner of the soil.

Besides the Smṛti literature and different commentaries we have the authority of foreign travellers and historians who unanimously testified the royal ownership of land. There is confusion regarding the translation of Strabo's statement. Prof. Ghoshal[2] and others have accepted Mr. Monahan's translation. But Dr. Barnett[3] has challenged the validity of this translation. Prof. Breloer[4] has suggested a new translation of the text which runs as "The whole of the land is the property of the king and the husbandman tills it on the condition of paying one-fourth of the produce." This statement of Strabo is in approximate agreement with that of Diodorus who stated that : "For the whole land they pay rent to the king, since all India is royal land no man of private station is permitted to possess any ground and apart from the rental they pay a fourth part into the royal treasury." This statement of Diodorus[5] is significant from different points of view.

1. *Bṛhas.*, xix, 22, 23.
2. *Hindu Revenue System*, p. 164.
3. *J.R.A.S.*, 1931, p. 166.
4. *Kauṭalīya-Studien*, vol. i, p. 54.
5. Diodorus Siculus, Book ii, pp. 23-24 (L.C.S.)

Firstly it states that nobody in India was allowed to possess private land. People used to get land from the king on lease and pay the normal rent. In addition to this rent the king used to realise an extra tax on agriculture, the existence of which can be corroborated by the occurrenee of the word *uparikara* in many of the inscriptions belonging of our period. Arrian's[1] reference to this effect is also significant, because he stated that the peasants pay tribute to the king or to the autonomous cities. There is no reference to private landlords or anything of the kind.

Fa-hsien[2] stated : "The people are numerous and happy: they have not to register their household or to attend to any magistrates and their rules : only those who cultivate the royal land have to pay (a portion of the gain from it)". Fa-hsien writes of the prosperity of the people and states that land is owned by the king but does not say a word about the individual ownership of land. We suggest that Fa-hsien employed the word 'royal land' for the whole of the cultivable land in the middle kingdom and thought that the king was its owner.

Hiuen-Tsiang stated[3] that : "Of the royal land there is a four-fold division, one part is for the endowment of great public servant, one to reward high intellectual eminence, one for acquiring religious merit by gifts of the various sects. The king's tenants pay one-sixth of the produce as rent". Two different interpretations have been made of this statement. Prof. Altekar[4] does not take it as clear evidence of royal ownership of land, while Prof. Ghoshal[5] stated : "This may be taken to imply that as in contemporary China the state of India was held to be owner of land". It may be objected against the latter interpretation that Hiuen-Tsiang has never referred to China in this context. On the other hand he referred to several divisions of land, but did not say a word about the possession of land by ordinary people.

1. *Indica*, ii, 9-10.
2. *Fa-Hsian's Record of the Buddhist Kingdom*, by J. Legge, p. 42.
3. *On Hiuen-Tsiang*, vol. i, p. 176, Watter's translation.
4. *S.G.A.I.*, p, 199, f. n. 5.
5. *A.S,A.I.*, p. 98.

Moreover the proportion of one-sixth mentioned by Hiuen-Tsiang as paid by tenants of the royal land is the same as that generally mentioned in the smṛtis as the general land tax of the whole kingdom. Thus it appears from the context that the royal ownership of land was so well recognised in our period that Hiuen-Tsiang thought it unnecessary to write about the types of settlement between the people and the king.

Besides this we have the authority of Kalhaṇa[1], who, writing about king Jayāpīda of Kashmir, stated that : "In his persistent greed he went so far in cruelty that for the three years he took the whole harvest, including the cultivators' share". It may be argued that the king did this purely out of greed. But this confiscation of the whole harvest from the farmers suggests that the king looked on himself as the owner of the entire land and thus thought that he was entitled to realise the revenue according to his discretion. Kalhaṇa further observed about king Śreṣṭhasena[2] : "That he looked upon the earth which was subject to his sway, as if it were the court of his palace." The same king, a benevolent and peaceful monarch whom Kalhaṇa greatly admired, is referred to in the following verse as "the lord of those kings who are family heads of the fields of the whole earth (*niḥśeṣa-Kṣmā-kedāra-Kuṭumbinām*). The last phrase evidently implies that Kalhaṇa looked on the king as the owner of the whole land in the same manner as a house-holder owns the family property. The choice of the word *kuṭumbin* in this connection incidentally perhaps implies that Kalhaṇa felt that as the head of the family controlled the family property in the interests of the family as a whole, so the king should govern in the interests of his subjects, but this is not immediately relevant to our purpose.

The king's undisputed authority over land can be gathered from the usual formulae of the many donative inscriptions of our period—for example Plates of the time of Śaśāṅkarāja[3]

1. Lobhābhyāsāttathā krauryaṁ sa yayau vatsaratrayam l
Saha kārṣakabhāgena yathāhārṣīccharataphalam ll
Rāja., vi, 628.

2. Gṛhāṅganamiva kṣoṇiṃ gaṇayanvaśavartinīm l Trigartorvīṃ grāma-madhye pravareśāya yo dadau ll 100 ll Iśo nṛpāṇām niḥśeṣakṣmā-kedārakuṭumbinām l Sa samāstriṃśataṃ bhūbhṛdanistriṃśāśayo'bhavat ll 100 ll *Rājā.*, 3.

3. *E. I.*, vol. vi, p. 145, lines 18-23.

state that the subordinate king, Mahāraja Mahāsāmanta Mādhavarāja II, "being in the good health suitably worships and honours princes, ministers, officers and their subordinates and others who are present or shall be present at the village of Chavalakhya which belongs to Kṛṣṇagiriviṣaya and informs them as follows :—'Let it be known to you that for the sake of our father and mother and for the increase of (our) own merit, with libation of water, at an eclipse of the sun, we granted (*pratipādita*) the village, to last for the same time as the sun and moon to Charpaṇasvāmi who belongs to the *gotra* of Bhāradvāja (and) has the *pravara* of Angirasa and Bārhaspatya'. The Madhuban copperplate grant of Harṣavardhana reads :[1] "Be it known to you that this village of Somakuṇdikā has been enjoyed (*bhukta*) by the brāhmaṇa Vāmarathya on the strength of a forged edict (*kūṭaśāsana*); having therefore broken that edict and confiscated (*ākṣipya*) the village from him, I have granted (*pratipādita*) it up to his boundaries, together with the right of all the income which ought to accrue to the house of the king, endowed with all immunities...... (with the right of) inheritance of sons and grandsons (for a period) lasting as long as moon, sun and earth endure, according to the maxim concerning land unfit for tillage, for the increase of merit and the fame of my father......"

References to this effect are so numerous that it seems unnecessary to count them all here. But it is quite clear from these citations that nobody in the villages in question was possessed of the right of full individual ownership of land. If there had been any such persons either the king would have mentioned their names and possessions or some sort of settlement with them would have been made before the donation. Thus the lack of such references in these royal grants suggests that the king was possessed of the whole land of the kingdom.

Hence, it would not be unreasonable to agree with V.A. Smith[2], who held that agricultural land was generally regarded as crown property in India of the period. It would appear,

1. *E.I.*, vol. i, p. 73, lines 10-15.
2. *Early History of India*, p. 131 (third edition)

however, that some Mimāṃsā theorists, who were specially devoted to the study of the Vedas, would never admit the king's ownership, as indeed they could not do, without rejecting or explaining away the ancient Vedic story of Viśvakarman Bhauvana, which from their point of view was divinely revealed and absolutely true. But by most of the authorities and probably by all the king of our period the reproof of the angry Earth Goddess was conveniently forgotten.

Chapter VII

DIPLOMATIC ORGANISATION AND THE POLICY OF PEACE IN EARLY MEDIEVAL INDIA

International law plays a very important part in modern inter-state relationship. S.V. Vishwanath[1] has attempted to find the existence of international law in ancient India in the following words : "Since international law, as law in general in India, has its origin in *dharma* it may be said that all the Aryan states were bound to observe the various rules of *dharma* in peace and war". But since we know that the *Smṛti* laws were meant for the Hindus only and India was connected with non-Hindu kingdoms such as Persia, the Roman empire and other countries from the earliest days to our period, it seems very hard to believe that non-Hindu travellers, merchants and others observed the Hindu Code of *dharma*. Similarly, it would be unreasonable to think that the orthodox Hindus followed the non-Hindu laws of social conduct in the foreign countries. Moreover, even amongst the Hindu kingdoms customs and manners differed from place to place, and we are told that traditions had priority over the *Smṛti* laws as can be gathered from the statement of Śukra[2]. "Those customs that have been introduced in the country, caste or race should be maintained in the same condition, for otherwise people get agitated". Further-more, the word *dharma* has been generally employed by *Smṛti* writers[3] in the sense of divinely ordained duty, whether applying to all men or particular groups. Therefore, it seems very unreasonable to hold on the basis of the widespread con cept of *dharma* that something like international law existed in ancient India.

Similarly it would be fallacious to state that anything like

1. *International Law in Ancient India*, p. 20.
2. *Śukra*, iv, Sec. v. 93.
3. *Manusmṛti*, vii. 144.

international interdependence was realised by the ancient Indians because "the recognition of international interdependence is comparatively new, in any systematic fashion it can hardly be dated earlier than the treaty of Versailles in 1919"[1].

Undoubtedly we have references to the effect that Indian merchants sailed to different ports of Asia and Africa, but the main articles of Indian trade were spices, ivory and similar other things[2] while India imported slaves, dancing girls, topaz, carbuncle etc. from the outer world.[3] These subjects of trade can be termed in modern phraseology luxury goods, without which a country can well survive. Moreover, we have no reference to the feverish competition for markets, or to traders looking back to their home government for protection of their trade. Wherever Indians went, they found an open market and so they made easy money.[4] Nor do we hear anything about an international body that guaranteed the security of the interests of every nation. We have reference to the formation of the *mandala*, but that is altogether a different concept, as we shall see later. Thus it would not be unreasonable to state that ancient Indians did not have any concept of the international interdependence, which is another important factor of the inter-state relationship of the politics of modern days.

In this connection it must be, however, admitted that the rulers of ancient India guaranteed security to foreign traders, because we have several references to this effect. Thus Merutuṅgācārya[5] states that king Vikramārka of Avanti bought an iron statue from a foreign merchant, who requested the king as follows : "Lord, having heard that goods are sold very quickly in your territory, I came here to this city and took this statue to different places. But people instead of buying it have insulted me......" Having considered this

1. *Laski, An Introduction to Politics*, p. 92.
2. *Mookherjee, Indian Shipping*, p. 148.
3. *Warmington, The Commerce between the Roman Empire and India*, p. 261 ff.
4. *Forbes, Rāsa Mālā*, p. 418.
5. *P.C.*, p., 5.

incident blameworthy the king paid a hundred thousand *dīnārs* to the trader, bought the statue and put it in the royal tresury. This implies that it was regarded as bad for the kingdom that a foreign merchant should return without selling his goods, and suggests that the king was responsible for the care of such merchants. The security of trade can be gathered from the following statement of Kalhaṇa.[1] "Padmarāja a foreigner, who supplied betel-leaves, was a favourite of this (king) (Ananta), who was lavish and fond of the habit of taking betel. It was through this (man) that Bhoja, the Lord of Mālwa, had the round tank (kuṇḍa) constructed at Kapateśvara with heaps of gold that he sent. King Bhoja had vowed that he would always wash his face in water from the Pāpasūdana Tīrtha, and this (man) made the filfulment of his difficult vow (possible) by regularly despatching from this (Tīrtha) large numbers of glass jars filled with that water. This man who sold betel-leaves with Nāgarakhaṇḍa and other (ingredients), made the king then give up almost the whole revenue of the country. As the king's creditor, he took from him a diadem which was adorned with five resplendent crescents, and the throne, as a security for more money which was due to him. In every month on the day of solemn reception, these emblems of regal dignity were brought from his house to be used in the royal assembly. The queen Sūryamatī then put an end to this disgrace caused to the country by Padmarāja, by handing over the savings of her own treasury". This statement of Kalhaṇa suggests that there was security of trade in the country even under weak kings. Traders did not have to fear that they would incur loss in foreign territories. In cases of their inability to sell expensive goods a good king held himself responsible for it. When people failed to pay in cash the price was paid in kind, that is to say, traders used to accept land and other commodities in return of their goods. The security of trade in our period can also be gathered from the statement of Muslim historian Al-Idrīsī[2], who, writing about the Cālukya kingdom, noted that "the town of Naharwāra is frequented by a large number of Musal-

1. *Rāja*, 7, 190-7.
2. *History of India*, by, Elliot and Dowson, vol, 1. p. 88,

man traders who go there on business." Had there been no security of trade the Muslim traders would have seldom ventured to trade with the Hindu kingdoms.

Hence it would not be unreasonable to suggest that though nothing like international law or the modern concept of international interdependence existed in ancient India, yet the Indian rulers offered security to foreign travellers and traders in our period. Relying upon the authority of Megasthenes, Mr. Vishvanatha[1] stated that of various departments of Candragupta Maurya's administration, one was alloted to the entertainment of foreigners. The officers of this department assigned lodgings to foreigners and kept watch over their modes of life by means of those persons whom they gave to them for assistance. They escorted them on the way when they left the country or in the event of their dying, forwarded their property to their relatives. They took care of them when they were sick and if they died buried them. Unfortunately we have no record to testify to the existence of similar officials in our period. But there are references which suggest that foreigners were welcomed in the country and that the security of their lives and property was guaranteed. For example Al-Idrīsī[2], referring to the ports of Gujarāt, stated that "they (the Musalmans) are honourably received by the king and his ministers and find protection and security". We should note Bṛhaspati's statement that brāhmaṇas and others belonging to another country should be welcomed in the country as though they were its own people[3]. The concluding statement of Śukra is not very clear in this respect, because he used the word travellers in a general sense. So it cannot be said with certainty whether the word has been used for the people of king's own kingdom or foreigners. However he stated[4] that "the master of the sarāi is to ask

1. *International Law in Ancient India*, pp. 53 ff. based on Strabo. xv, 1, 50.
2. *History of India*, by Elliot and Dowson, vol. i, p. 88.
3. *Bṛhaspati Arthaśāstra* III, 51-52.
4. Tatrāgataṃ tu sampṛechet pānthaṃ śālādhipassadā l
Prayāto' si kutaḥ kasmāt kva gacchasi ṛtaṃ vada ll
Sasahāyo, sahāyo vā saśastraḥ kim savāhanaḥ l
Kā jātiḥ kiṃ kulaṃ nāma sthitiḥ kutrāsti te ciram ll

the following question from the traveller coming to it : Whence are you coming and why? Whither are you going? Have you any arms in your possession and have you conveyances with you? What is your caste? What are your family and name? Where is your permanent residence? Asking these questions the master of the sarāi should note them down in the evening, and having taken away the traveller's arms, should advise him 'take sleep carefully'. Having counted the number of the men in the house and shut its gate, he should have it watched by guards working for three hours each and awaken the men in the morning. He should give back the men his arms, count the men and then let them go by opening the gate, and a villager should accompany them to the boundary". This is somewhat similar to the statement of Megasthenes that we have already seen above. But it is by no means clear that in the case of a foreigner's death his belongings were sent back to his people and his body was disposed of. But it is to be noted that the care of the travellers in this way evidently had a further motive than mere hospitality—namely the keeping of a check on their numbers and movements in order to avoid crime.

Prof. Altekar[1], Dr. A.K. Majumdar[2] and Dr. H. Chatterjee[3] have contended that passports were issued to permit travel to different kingdoms, and Prof. Majumdar has suggested that it was the function of the Cālukya Mahāmātya to issue passports. We have certainly clear indication to this effect in the Mauryan period, but none of the texts of our period, such as the *Agni Purāṇa*, *Śukranītisāra*, *Kāmandakanītisāra* etc., refer to this function of the *amātya*. The *Mudrā* of which the Cālukya

Iti pṛṣṭvā likhet sāyam śastraṃ tasya pragṛhya ca l
Sāvadhānamanā bhūtvā svāpam kurviti śāsayet ll
Tatrasthān gaṇayitvā tu śālādvāram pidhāya ca l
Samraksayedyānikaiśca prabhāte tān prabodhayet l
Śastram dadyācca gaṇayeddvāramudghāṭya mocayet l
Kurayāt sahāyaṃ sīmāntāṃ teṣāṃ grāmyajanassadā l
Śukra. I. 540-49.

1. *S.G.A.I.*, p. 221.
2. *Cālukyas of Gujarat*, p. 222.
3. *International Law & Interstate Relations in Ancient India*, p. 66.

minister had charge was probably a royal seal. There are a number of foreign travellers who visited different parts of the country during our period, such as Hiuen Tsiang, Suleiman the Merchant, and others, but none of them have referred to such things. There is a reference to this effect in Merutuṅgācārya[1], who states that king Bhīma of Gurajat sent his envoy named Dāmara to king Bhoja of Mālwa, with a document bearing the royal seal. The document carried the instructions to Bhoja to kill the envoy. A royal credential or passport is issued for the protection of the bearer, and certainly not for his slaughter. Therefore, it would be very objectionable to take this example as evidence for existence of passport. Hence, in the absence of any evidence, it seems very difficult to believe that anything like a passport or visa system was prevalent in the India of our period.

Similarly it would be wrong to assume that anything like modern diplomatic services existed in India in our period. If it were asked whether permanent ambassadors existed in ancient India or not, the answer would be in the negative : the creation of this office is a fairly recent development. But it is clear that envoys were often despatched by different rulers of the time. Several authors of the period have thrown light upon this matter. Śukra presented other authorities' views as well as his own. Commenting upon these he stated that[2] "the king is said always to have eight elements of regal administration (in place of the usual seven) according to some people...The envoy who is well versed (in the art of reading) emotions and gestures (expression) is a companion of these (as the eighth)". This implies that the office of the envoys was next to the first seven important departments of the kingdom and the envoys were among the most important of the royal officers. But according to Śukra's own view envoys were tenth because he stated[3] : "The priest is superior

1. *Punaḥ kautukākṣiptacittaḥ śrī-Bhīmaḥ kasminnavasare mudrāmudrita-lekham vidhāya taddhaste samarpya, upadāpāṇiṃ taḍḍāmaraṃ Mālave' praiṣīt* l P. C., 34.

2. Aṣṭa prakṛtibhiryukto nṛpaḥ kaiscitsmṛtassadā l
Ingitākāratattvajño dūtastadanugassmṛtaḥ ll *Śukra*, ii, 145-149.

3. Purodhāḥ prathamam Śreṣṭhaśsarvebhyo rājarāṣṭrabhṛt l
Dūtastataḥ kramādete pūrvaṣreṣṭhā yathāgunaḥ ll
Śukra, ii, v. 1-0-155.

to all others—the mainstay of the kingdom and the king. The viceroy comes next, next the premier, then the *saciva* then the minister, next the justice, then the scholar, next comes *sumantra*, then the *amātya*, lastly the envoy; these officers are successively meritorious in order." Besides Śukra none of the other authors of the period give any indications on the matter. Therefore, we cannot say anything with certainty as to what position they held in the royal court. But it is clear from almost every source that *dūtas* were appointed from respectable families. Thus Somadeva[1] stated that men free from vices, eloquent scholars, influential, who could understand the feelings of others, loyal and born of high family, should be appointed as envoys. Lakṣmīdhara, agreeing with Manu[2], held : "As envoy he (king) shall appoint one who is well-versed in all the sciences, who understands hints, expressions and gestures, who is honest, expert and born of high family. That royal envoy is commended who is loyal, honest, clever, possessed of good memory, conversant with place and time, handsome of body, fearless and eloquent". The *Agni Purāṇa*[3] stated that : "A man, intelligent, ingenious, well-versed in the arts of war and scriptural knowledge and accustomed to work of espionage and possessing a good retentive memory and eloquence of speech, should be appointed as the envoy". Caṇḍeśvara[4] held the same view as Lakṣmīdhara. An analysis of the above mentioned authors' statements suggests that loyalty and birth in a high family were not the only qualification of envoys, but they had to be intelligent and eloquent in deposition.

Both the *Agni Purāṇa*[5] and Somadeva[6] stated that there were three different types of envoys, i.e. *Niḥśṛṣṭārtha, Mitārtha* and *Śāsanāhāra.* On the power of the envoys the *Agni Purāṇa* agrees with Kāmandaka and states that the *Niḥśṛṣṭārtha* was to be entrusted with the management of an affair according

1. *N.V.*, 13, 4, p. 170.
2. *Kṛtyakalpa.*, ch. iv, p. 33.
3. *Agni.*, ch. 241, v. 7.
4. *R.N.*, p. 42.
5. *Agni.*, ch. 241, v. 8.
6. *N.V.*, ch, 13, p. 170.

to his own light and discretion, (2) the *Mitārtha* was charged with the execution of a mission according to the directions received from his sovereign (8) the *Śāsanahāraka's* duty was only to deliver the message of his master on a particular question.

Regarding the despatch of envoys authorities[1] unanimously held that they should be previously acquainted with the countries where they were expected to go.

Success of the embassy largely depended upon the behaviour of the envoys. Both Lakṣmīdhara[2] and Caṇḍeśvara, agreeing with Manu, held that peace or war depend upon the envoy. Commenting upon the same verse of Manu, Medhātithi[3] stated that the envoy brings about the alliance of kings, and also disunites those already united. He does the former by saying even such agreeable things as he has not been commissioned to say; and the latter by describing even such unfriendly acts as may not have been done, and by not paying the presents of gold and other things that he may have brought with him. In this way he disunites allies. Thus duties assigned to the *dūtas* are of temporary nature. Therefore, it seems that missions were sent to different countries from time to time and there is no evidence to the permanent emmissaries in our period.

The next question is—what sort of relations were to be maintained by the different rulers of the period and what were these messages that the envoys had to carry ?

Authorities may argue that interstate relationships in India were relationships of war and conquest. But the existence of such attitudes has been challenged by authorities on ancient India such as Prof. Altekar,[4] Indra,[5] Mr. Visvanath[6] and Dr. Chatterjee.[7] Prof. Altekar relying upon the authority

1. *Agni.*, ch. 241, v. 8.
2. *Kām.*, xii, v. 3, *Agni.* ch. 241, v.
3. *Kṛtyakalpa.*, p. 33.
   R.N., p. 42.
4. *S.G.A.I.*, p. 217.
5. *Ideologies of War & Peace in Ancient India*, pp. 99 ff.
6. *International Law in Ancient India*, p. 110.
7. *International Law and Interstate Relations in Ancient India*, p. 71.

of Manu and Kāmandaka has stated : "Almost all of them (the text books) pointed out to the ambitious king that the appeal to the arms should be avoided as far as possible; an unrighteous war promotes infamy in this life and procures hell thereafter." S.V. Visvanath, on the authority of the *Mahābhārata*, stated that "it is stated definitely that war should be waged only if all other expedients of bringing about peace have failed". The statements of these authorities can be strengthened by the following extracts from different sources of our period. Kāmandaka stated that "The sovereign who desires to reach the aim of prosperity should make peace even with one equal to him in all respects. Indian authors have propounded four different means of diplomacy, i.e. *Sāma* (appeasement), *dāna* (gift), *daṇḍa* (force) and *bheda* (sowing dissension). The policy of *sāma* was recommended to be adopted in the following words : "We should not mutually injure each other but should rather help each other in time of need. This peace should be made even with the greatest enemies.[1] The *Agni Purāṇa* gives seven different modes of diplomacy (adding three others to the traditional four), *Sāma, dāna, bheda, daṇḍa, upekṣā* (inactivity), *māyā* (delusion), and *indrajāla* (magic)[2] and while discussing the different modes of diplomacy it treats *sāma* first, which may be an indication that the policy of appeasement was to be followed first. Commenting upon Manu, Medhātithi[3] suggested that "he (the king) shall not go to war in a hurry. At first he shall try conciliation. i.e. friendly meeting, sitting together, conversing, seeing each other's wife and so forth". Thus our authors advised the king to adopt the policy of conciliation first in the international affairs. The same attitude of Hindu diplomacy can be attested from the Jaina and Buddhist literature.

The Buddhist text *Suvarṇabhāsottama Sūtra* gives the massage

---

1. *Parasparamaniṣṭaṃ na cintanīyaṃ tvayā mayā* l
susāhāyyam hi kartavyamiti śatrau prakīrtitam ll
Śukra, iv. i, 61-62.

2. *Agni.*, ch. 241, v. 46-47.

3. *Na sahasā yudhyeta* l *Etāvatprathamam*
visiṣṭasthāpanopadesanaṃ sumukham ca mitho
sahāsanakathāsahadāradarśanādi ll Medhātithi on Manu vii,198.

of the heavenly Buddha to the divine kings of the Four Quarters in the following words : "Protect all these royal families, cities and provinces, cherish them, ward off invasion from them, give them peace and prosperity, keep them free from all fear, calamity and evil portent. Turn back the troops of their enemies and create in all the earthly kings of India a desire to avoid fighting, attacking, quarrelling or disputing with their neighbours...When eighty-four thousand cities of India are contended with their own territories and with their kingly state and their own hoards of treasure, they will not attack one another or raise mutual strife. They will gain their thrones by the due accumulation of the merits of former deeds, they will be satisfied with their own kingly state and will not destroy one another nor show their mettle by laying waste whole Provinces. When all the eighty four thousand kings of eighty-four thousand cities of India think of their mutual welfare and feel mutual affection and joy... contended in their own domains. —India will be prosperous, well-fed, pleasant and populous. The earth will be fertile and the months and seasons and years will all occur at the right time-planets and moon and sun will duly bring on the days and nights. Rain will fall upon earth at the proper time. And all living beings in India will be rich with all manner of riches and corn, very prosperous (but) not greedy.[1]

Somadeva[2] has thrown useful light upon the matter. He states : "Politics and valour of kings are for winning the world, not abandoning it. Only the king who cannot conquer his neighbour in a war of wits starts up a war of weapons. For arrows are not as powerful as wisdom of wise...Even when he sees it, the arrows of the archer may miss the target but the wise man has the skill to hit the mark even when he cannot see it. The wisdom of the wise is an unfailing weapon.

1. I am very thankful to Prof. Basham, who allowed me to use his translation of the text.

2. Tāni ca rājakulāni tāni ca nagarāni tāni ca rāṣṭrāṇi tāni ca viṣayaṇyārakṣayiṣvatha paritrāṇaṃ parigrahaṃ paripālanaṃ daṇḍaparihāraṃ śāntiṃ svastyāyanaṃ karisyatha, Sarvajambudvipagatāni ca sattvāni sarvadhana dhāṇyasamṛddhānibhaviṣyanti mahābhogāni cāmatrāṇi ca bhavisyanti S. Śūtra, vi. pp. 73-75.

A king struck down by wisdom is as though struck by thunderbolts and will never rise again. The over-aggressive (*atitīkṣṇa*) king, though he be strong, is as a grasshopper and will not be happy for long. But when death is equally probable whether one strikes or runs away it is better to strike than merely to perish...Adventure undertaken without knowing one's strength is like trying to crack a mountain with one's head. The force of arms cannot do what peace does. If you can gain your desired end with sugar why use poison ?... What sensible man will abandon his bale (of merchandise) for fear of having to pay toll in it ? When the water is drained from the lake the crocodile grows as thin as a snake. A lion when he leaves the forest is no more than a jackal. And a snake whose fangs are drawn is a mere rope. In union is strength. Even a mad elephant will trip in a twisted clump of grass. And the Elephants of the Four Quarters are held by twisted fibers. But what is the use of other means when they (enemy) can only be put down by force ? Such expedients are like a libation of ghee on the fire".

In the *Yaśastilaka*,[1] it has been stated that the king should dwell upon the policy of peace rather than waging war. There is a reference to the same effect in the *Laghvarhannīti*[2].

Śukra[3] stated at one place that enemies are to be destroyed by the policy of alliance as well as by other three means. Thus friendship was considered as better means for destroying enemies than anything else. This friendship (*Sāma*) has been devided into two categories namely (1) *Satyasāma* and (2) *asatyasāma* in the *Matsya Purāṇa*.[4] The policy of *asatyasāma* may have been meant for treacherous fellows but it was in no case to be applied to a true friend. And since, it was only the policy of *satyasāma* which was advised to be applied in case of true ally.

Present (*dānam*) was considered as one of the important means for winning friendship by the author of our period. Thus we find Śukra[5] stating that a king should win over his

1. *Yaśastilaka.*, III, pp. 375-95.
2. *Laghvarhannīti.*, II. 1. 19-30.
3. *Śukra* iv sec. I, v, 47.
4. *Mat.*, ch. 222, v. 4-7.
5. *Śukra.*, iv Sec. 1, v. 73.

adversary by means of gifts. Medhātithi[1] commenting upon Manu made the same statement. According to him, the things being given as *dāna* were gold and similar other valueable objects. It was to be given as token of affection with ambition to create mental attachment. The *Agni Purāṇa*[2] referred to a few significant presents, which were bound to create good relations and they may be counted (1) making present of articles not previously offered to the other king (2) accepting things by the latter of his own choice (3) paying off tribute by a king due from him to his enemy or paramount and (4) setting at liberty prisoners captured in war. All these expedients were to be applied to make the enemy a good friend.

Application of above mentioned expedients with the enemies was expected to bring good result. In case these measures fail to bear fruit, rulers were advised to bring dissension in the enemy camp. Being scared of this measure, theoreticians thought, enemy would be forced to come on good terms with him and thus we find Śukra stating that dissension should be brought in the enemy camp and his life should be threatened. Commenting upon Manu, Medhātithi[3] held that effective dissension is possible only when the family members of the enemy go against him and the enemy starts looking at them with suspicion. *Agni Purāṇa*[4] refers to three different means of sowing dissensions in the enemy camp. They are counted as to destroy amity between two persons, secondly to producc thrill of fear between two persons, and lastly to induce a party to betray the secrets confined in him by the other. It was expected that these measures would bring disunity, people would not rely upon one another and a state of confusion would be raised in the enemy camp, In the meantime it was expected from the *Vijigīṣu* to establish his influence by other means. And thus the enemy would have no alternative left but to make alliance for prosperity with the *Vijigīṣu*.

1. *Medhātithi on Manu.*, vill. v. 198.
2. *Agni.*, ch. 241, ver. 50.
3. *Medhātithi on Manu,* vii, 198.
4. Agni., ch. 241, v. 56-51.

Thus we see that almost every device was framed to help the co-existence of nations and rulers were expected to rule in peace and prosperity. Even in case of failure of the above-mentioncd measure, rulers were advised not to plunge in war suddenly. In the name of peace and prosperity they were advised to keep silent and form alliances according to the age-old idea of *maṇḍala*. Entry into the *maṇḍala* would add moral strength to the king. Being thus strengthened one would be left in peace and rule happily.

Regarding the formation of *maṇḍala* we get varieties of informations in our period. The Hindu school of thought headed by Kāmandaka[1] and Medhātithi took the *Vijigīṣu*, *Ari*, *Udāsīna* and *madhyama* as the principal elements of the *maṇḍala* and the remaining eight as subsidiary, while the author of the *Agni Purāṇa*[2] and the Jaina author Somadeva did not make any such distinction. The later classification was based upon the ideologies of the ancient period when all of them were regarded important.

Whatever may have been the differences an analysis of them suggests that the universal *maṇḍala* was ideally formed in the following manner. The *Vijigīṣu* was regarded as in the centre, the neighbouring prince of *Vijigīṣu* was his enemy and the neighbouring prince of the enemy was the friend of the *Vijigīṣu*, the neighbouring prince of this ally was the friend of the enemy, the neighbouring prince of this prince was the friend of the friend and so on. This scheme applied in the front of the *manḍala*. There is a similar formation in the rear. Neighbouring prince in the rear was the *Pārṣṇigrāha* who was hostile to *Vijigīṣu*. The neighbouring prince of this prince was *Ākranda*, who was the friend of *Vijigīṣu*. The Ākranda's territory was bordered by that of the *Āsāra*, who was supposed to be the friend of *Pārṣnigrāha*, and the Āsāra's territory was contiguous to the territory of the *Ākrandāsāra*, who was supposed to be the ally of the *Ākranda*, and so on.

The *Madhyma* is the king whose territory is co-terminous with that of the king in question. The neutral (*Udāsīna*) is

1. *Kām.*, viii, 22, Medhātithi on Manu, vii, 156-7 & onwards.
2. *Agni.*, ch. 233, v. 13-19, N. V. p. 318 ff.

one who is capable of defeating each of the two. Both Kāmandaka[1] and Medhātithi stated that : "These twelve cardinal sovereigns together with their five respective *prakṛtis* (1) minister (2) kingdom (3) fortress (4) treasury (5) the army constitute the *prakṛti maṇḍala* of seventy-two elements".

Kāmandaka has gone deeper into the subject, and along with his own has presented the views of others regarding the formation of *manḍala.* He[2] states that a common enemy of the *Vījigīṣu,* the Ari and a common ally of them both these two, each of them again with an ally and an enemy of his own, together with twelve cardinal kings constitute the *maṇḍala* of eighteen monarchs mentioned by Guru (Bṛhaspati).

The six *prakṛtis* namely the minister, kingdom, castle, treasury, army and ally of each of these eighteen monarchs taken together, form the *maṇḍala* of one hundred and eight elements which has been recognised by the wise.

"These eighteen monarchs each with an ally and an enemy constitute the *maṇḍala* of fifty-four kings, spoken of by Viśālākṣa.

"The six *prakṛtis,* namely minister, kingdom, castle, treasury, army and ally, of each of these fifty-four kings taken together, again form the *maṇḍala* of three hundred and twenty-four elements.

"The seven constituents of the government of the *Vijigīṣn* together with the seven constituents of the *Ari,* constitute what is known as the *maṇḍala* of fourteen components.

"The *Vijigīṣu,* the *Ari* and the *Madhyama* form the *maṇḍala* of the kings. These three monarchs with an ally of each of them together constitute what others call the *maṇḍala* of six kings.

"The six *prakṛtis* namely minister etc. of each of these six kings taken together compose what persons conversant with the formation of *maṇḍala* designate as the *maṇḍala* of thirty-six parts.

---

1. *Kām.*, viii, v. 25, *Medhātithi on Manu*, vii, v. 157.

In this classification the seventh element of sovereignty, the ally (mitra) is omitted, for the obvious reasons that he is already a member of the *maṇḍala*.

2. *Kām.*, viii, 26.

"The seven constituents of *Vijigīṣu* those of the *Ari*, and those of the *Madhyama*, taken together constitute what other politicians call the *maṇḍala* of twenty-one elements.

"The four cardinal monarchs of a *maṇḍala* (viz. the *Vijigīṣu*, the *Ari*, the Madhyama and the Udāsīna), each with an ally of his own, become eight in number. These eight kings with their respective *prakṛtis*, minister etc., form the *maṇḍala* the number of whose components is as many as that of the syllables contained in a stanza composed in a *jagatī* metre[1].

"Those monarchs who are in the front of the *Vijigīṣu* and those who are in his rear together with himself, constitute the *maṇḍala* monarchs, spoken of by those who are acquainted with the nature of *maṇḍala*.

"An ally and an enemy in front of the *Vijigīṣu* also an ally and an enemy in his rear, together with himself form five in number. The six *prakṛtis*, namely minister etc. of the each of these five sovereigns, taken together, constitute what is recognised as the *maṇḍala* of thirty elements.

"Those best conversant with the *Śāstras* also recognise these *maṇḍalas* in respect of the *Ari*. The intelligent ascribe the *maṇḍala* of five kings and *maṇḍala* of thirty elements also to the *Ari*.

"Parāśara says that two *prakṛtis* only are to be recognised in polity; of them the important one is he who assists and the other is he who is assailed.

"In consequence of the *Vijigīṣu* and the *Ari* assailing each other, the relation of *Vijigīṣu* and *Ari* becomes interchangeable. And thus there appears to be one *prakṛti* only."

After the formation of the *maṇḍala* rulers were advised to ponder over the policy of alliance[2]. Thus it appears that formation of *maṇḍala* was mainly meant for avoiding the war—an idea which has been provided by N N. Law[3].

---

1. A kind of metre with twelve syllables to a quarter, so that the total number of syllables in a stanza is 48.

2. *Kām.*, viii, 47, *R.N.*, p. 56.
   N.V., p. 323.
   Aparārka on Yājña, I, 345.

3. *Inter-state relations in Ancient India*, pp. 8 ff.

The following measures were devised to avoid direct clash by Kāmandaka. He states[1] "The means for stopping the wars caused by the usurpation of kingdom, abduction of females, and seizure of provinces and portion of territory have been specified by those skilled in the expedients of policy, the restoration of females and the evacuation of the provinces respectively.

"The means of pacifying the wars caused by the violation of laws and the spoilation of property, are the restoration of the laws and the restitution of the property respectively. The means for putting an end to a war caused by the molestation of the kingdom by the foes is to molest the kingdom of the later in return.

"Of wars caused by the carrying away of treasures and by the destruction of knowledge and the prostration of the regal powers, the end is reached by the restitution of things taken, by the foreigners and indifference.

"Wars brought about by allies through their oppressions and persecution should be looked upon with indifference, but for a generous ally even the very life may be risked.

"War caused by the offer of insult should be extinguished by the offer of honour. Conciliation and propitiation are the means of pacifying a war caused by the pride and arrogance of one party.

"A brave king should reach the end of a war caused by the destruction of a friend or an ally by the application of underhand measures or by having recourse to incantation and magical spells.

"For pacifying a war which has for its cause the eagerness for possessing the same object (by two kings) a prudent king should give up that object provided that his royal prestige does not suffer thereby.

"A war caused by the spoilation of a portion of the treasures should not be prosecuted, inasmuch as, in carrying on such a war, the man may lose all the treasure.

"When the party against whom the war is waged is numerous, its end should be reached by sowing dissension in

---

1. *Kām.*, ch. x, v. 6-18.

the enemy's camp by gift, bribery, reconciliation, tempting offers and other such expedients of policy.

"War caused by the want of sowing compassion to creatures should be extinguished by speaking agreeable and pleasing words to them. The means approved by the pious for pacifying a war brought about by the evil influence of fate into propitiate fate.

War incident to the rebellion of the affected *maṇḍala* is to be pacified by the application of one or the other measures of the policy."

In case the above mentioned measures failed and war became inevitable Kāmandaka[1] suggests that a king should in no case be involved in such conflicts as the one in which the result is uncertain or the profit of victory is absolutely nil or very insignificant, a war which effects the existing order of things or vitiates the treatise in force at its outset and proves fruitless in the long run, or the one which affects the foreign relations of a king and brings on many an evil both at the beginning and in the end, or the one in which a foreign prince, of whose forces no correct estimate can be made, threatens to mobilise his armies for the assault of a war where contention is for the recovery of a kidnapped woman or of the fame of an insulted ally, or a long and tedious war with the brāhmaṇas. Similarly a king should not fight with an enemy backed by a mighty ally and equipped with the good graces of providence. A war that promises a little profit at the outset, but is sure to terminate in a wild goose chase as well as its contrary, should be avoided by all means".

Thus from the authorities quoted above it appears that war was looked as the last resort of early medieval Indian diplomacy and when it was felt necessary theorists advised rulers to wage war only when they were strong enough to do so, otherwise it would do them no good. Kāmandaka[2] stated that : When an intelligent monarch finds his own army happy and efficient and that of his in the reverse state, then he may launch upon war. When he finds his own *prakṛti maṇḍala* swelling the prosperity and very loyal to him, and that

1. *Kām.*, x, 9-23.
2. *Kām.*, x, 27-29.

of his enemy in the reverse conditions, then he may embark upon war.

Theoreticians[1] framed rules concerning war, military discipline, morality and several other aspects of war which it appears unnecessary to mention, because we are only concerned with the external affairs of the king here and nothing else.

After victory in war rulers were advised and expected to follow the following precepts which has been stated by Medhātithi[2] as : After the enemy has been defeated and quiet has been restored in the captured city and among the people, he shall worship the Gods and the righteous brāhmaṇas......For the safety of the householders, in order that their livelihood may not suffer, he shall remit such portions of the taxes as may be too burdensome for them, not realising them for one or two years. He shall make it known among the people of the city and the villages—by the beat of the drum or the falling of the mace and such other means—that what they had done by virtue of their loyalty to their former master had been forgiven and that henceforward, everyone of them was free to his own calling. If, even after bestowing such favours, he finds that the citizens and the people are so loyal to their former master that they still cherish feelings of attachment towards his dynasty and that any government of his own would not be lasting—then he shall do as follows. Having briefly ascertained that such and such is the wish of the citizens and other people—'they do not wish to be governed in such and such manner, they wish to have a king of the same family as their former ruler'—he shall set up a member of the same family, who may be mild-tempered and happy in his family surroundings and then conclude a treaty with the king thus set up along with his assembled subjects and ministers, the terms of treaty being—you and I shall have equal shares in your income, you shall consult me in all that you do or do not do at the proper time you shall come and help me with your treasury and forces and so forth".

---

1. *Śukra*, iv, Sec. II, Manu, vii, v. 181 onwards.
2. *Medhātithi on Manu*. vii, 201 onwards.

The above-mentioned statement suggests that it was realised that mere conquest in war would not bring peace. The conquerer was advised to satisfy the demands of his new subjects by worshipping their Gods, reducing burdensome taxes and granting amnesties. If even after this the subject preferred the rule of their former master, then the conquerer should bring one of the family members of the defeated king on the throne and make alliance with him that he would remain the faithful vassal of the conqueror.

A somewhat similar statement was made by Kātyāyana[1] who stated : "Even when the king is at fault, the (conqueror) should not ruin the country (for the vanquished king's fault) since the vanquished king does not start on his career of wrong-doing with the consent of the subjects.

The *Viṣṇu smṛti*[2] stated : "A king having conquered the capital of his foe, should invest there a prince of the royal race of that country with the royal dignity. Let him not extirpate the royal race, though the royal race be of ignoble descent.

Thus the statements of these two authors support Medhātithi's view that the interest of the people should not be put down and that the family members of the defeated king should be brought on the throne.

The testimony of these statements can be affirmed by the account of the foreign traveller Sulaiman the Merchant[3] who records : "When a king subdues a neighbouring state, he places over it a man belonging to the family of the fallen prince, who carries on the government in the name of the conqueror. The inhabitants do not suffer it to be otherwise".

These statements are worth comparison with a passage of Machiavelli's which treats of the three means of ruling conquered countries.

The third[4] is to permit them (the conquered people) to live under their own laws, drawing a tribute and establishing within it an oligarchy which will keep it friendly to you. Because such a government, being created by the prince,

1. *Kāt.*, 21.
2. *Viṣṇu*, ch. iii, ver. 47-49.
3. *History of India by Elliot & Dowson*, vol. 1. p. 7.
4. *The Prince*, ch. 5, p. 25 (Everyman's Library series 1952).

knows that it cannot stand without his friendship and interest and does its utmost to support him; and therefore, he who would keep a city accustomed to freedom will hold it more easily by the means of its own citizens than in any other way".

Finally, Medhātithi[1] states : "All the customs relating to the property of brāhmaṇas or temples and to the duties of the people they may have been prevalent in the kingdom from before—all those he shall confirm, and make 'authoritative' By so doing, they become attached to him; and the leading men that may be there; their importance being due to their being rich in their belongings in the size of their family and such other qualifications, along with these, the new king shall be honoured with presents of weapons, money, grain, ornaments, conveyances, umbrella, throne, crown and so forth". There is a similar statement made by Kātyāyana[2] : "Whatever (gift) a king offers in a proper manner to a suppliant without distress (to himself), that gift saves him; such a gift made for the purpose of (accumulating) merit becomes enduring (in its result)", which implies that the conquerer, having made donations to suitable persons in the conquered country, wins their confidence and they in return accept the suzerainty of the conqueror.

Thus we see that though ahead of their time, Indian theoriticians advised their king to maintain friendly relation with all and to remain satisfied with what they had. In case of threat, they were advised to join the *maṇḍala* and to live in peace and prosperity. War was regarded as the end of Indian diplomacy. Rulers were expected to wage war only when they were strong enough to subdue the enemy. In the conquered country rulers were suggested to care for the interest and sentiments of the vanquished.

1. *Medhātithi on Manu*, vii, 203.
2. *Kāt.*, ver. 22.

Chapter VIII

CONCLUSION

This brings us to the close of our study of kingship in early mediaeval India. We have consulted many different sources, including Hindu, Jaina, and Buddhist texts, epigraphic records and foreign accounts, but we have found very little originality in the political ideas of the period. The *Yukti-kalpataru* and *Śukranītisāra* amongst the Hindu sources appear to be the most original contributions of the period. But even in these writings we find that their authors were inspired almost entirely by the ancient Hindu ideologies. Of most of the Hindu authors it can be stated with confidence that they had no originality whatever. Their political doctrines were propounded long before their time and in many cases they have quoted passages from ancient sages in their support. A decline is evident in the Buddhist sources. It appears that the Buddhists of the period had largely forgotten their own approach to politics and followed the political ideology of the Hindus. Jainas were too simple in their political outlook to formulate really individual views of their own, and therefore they also followed the old Hindu ideas of politics with slight variations.

The Hindus and Jainas had, however, different views about the origin of the kingship. According to the Hindu[1] theorists God created kings for the benefit of his creation, while the Jainas[2] narrated a story of the origin of kingship which suggests the survival of memories of primitive conditions rather like those in parts of nineteenth century Africa, where magicians were found to be also kings and were thought to benefit the people in both capacities. There is no reflection of the doctrines of the origin of kingship through social contract in the Buddhist sources nearest to our period, and the account

1. *Supra.*
2. *Supra.*

of kingship that we are given in the *Suvarṇabhāsottama Sūatra*[1] maintains its divine origin Thus we see that by far the greater number of the Indians in our period believed in the divine origin of kingship.

In spite of differences of opinion about the origin of kingship, authors of the period, though belonging to different sects, generally accepted the divinity of the king[2]. They thought that the king was sacred because he was composed of the particles of different gods. He became an embryo in the womb of a royal mother by the command of gods and was thus born as mortal. He was the favourite son of Heaven and it was through His good will that favourable winds blew, rain fell in season, planets, stars, sun and moon were auspicious, and corn, flowers, fruits and seed ripened properly. Hence in the name of God and prosperity, even an infant king was to be honoured and his commands were never to be disobeyed.

The king was possessed[3] of political, social, economic, religious and judicial authority in his kingdom. He had councillors and advisers whom he consulted on every important matter, but it was up to him to follow their advice or not, as he thought fit. Nowhere is the king described as bound to put the advice of these advisers into practice, and we have seen that on many occasions these kings acted quite independently of councillors[4] and others. Similarly, there is no reference to the effect that these councillors normally effectively opposed the king's will. On the other hand we have reference to councillors who are described as giving their approval[5] to the royal command without any consideration, and who are emphatically praised for their unquestioning obedience. The king, being free from the fear of opposition, generally acted autocratically and often troubled his subjects.

There were rulers who failed to perform the innumerable royal duties that were prescribed by the ancient sages for

1. *Supra*,
2. *Supra*,
3. *Supra*,
4. Supra,
5. Supra,

the benefit of the people and the kingdom in general. Instead of giving donations and constructing temples some of them even confiscated their valuables and realised taxes on goods meant to be used by gods and temples[1]. Brāhmaṇas were sometimes insulted and refugees were not given asylum.[2] *Varṇāśrmadharma*[3] was not always maintained properly and intermixing of castes was not unknown[4]. On the other hand many of the kings[5] of our period constructed canals, dams, etc. for irrigation purposes, and encouraged agriculture. They worshipped the gods[6] and made donations to religious causes[7] with open hands. They invited scholars to their courts[8], held religious conferences and encouraged philosophical studies by giving grants to learned men. The fact that there are so many examples of both good and bad kings is evidence of the king's absolute authority. Thus we conclude that if the king was good, attempts were made to carry out the royal functions as laid down in the *smṛtis*, at least to a certain extent, and if otherwise, the people had to face all kinds of troubles from the ruler. Neither did the people have the constitutional right to oppose the king nor did they offer any effective resistance to the king's commands, and kings generally ruled according to their own consciences.

Rulers of the period regarded the agricultural land as their ancestral property.[9] There was nothing to stop these rulers from dispossessing their tenants. They did not allow tenants to hand over lands occupied by them to anybody without royal permission.[10] They often increased the land revenue according to their needs and harassed people in its realisation. In cases of failure of the payment of royal revenue they dispossessed peasants from the whole of the land held by them.[11]

---

1. Supra,
2. Supra,
3. Supra,
4. Supra,
5. Supra,
6. Supra,
7. Supra,
8. Supra,
9. Supra,
10. Supra,
11. Supra,

Both international law and the concept of international interdependence were non-existent.[1] There was no committee of nations to safeguard the interest of smaller countries. But these rulers encouraged foreign trade and guarded the interests of the merchants[2]. They also extended security of life and prosperity to the travellers. Consequently, several travellers of eminence visited India and left valuable records of their impressions for later historians.

Political theorists of the period emphasised the utility of maintaining friendly relations with all countries, even with potential[3] enemies. In case the policy of peace failed, the kings were advised to make every effort to discover the secrets of the enemy and to bring about dissension in his court. When the enemy was weakened kings were advised to march against him. If the enemy was defeated his territory was to be annexed by the conquerer. But if the subjects of the defeated kings were not prepared to tolerate the foreign yoke, in that case it was demanded of the conqueror to bring one of the family members of the defeated king to the throne and make alliance with him that he would remain faithful and loyal to the conqueror[4].

This trend of Indian thought on politics is very near to the political philosophy of Dante[5] who thought that the peace and prosperity of mankind could be achieved only under a king. It is only in the king that the unity of human nature and human destiny can be duly expressed. It is only in the king that the final court of appeal can be found. The maintenance of justice is dependent upon the king's power and will. The king as the head is possessed of the absolute power of the kingdom and as an absolute king he can maintain justice. Real liberty can be found only in monarchy. The concord of will that is essential for the peace and happiness of mankind can only be insured by the dominance of one will, that is the monarch. The king will safeguard the interests of the

1. Supra.
2. Suprā.
3. Supra.
4. Supra.
5. *Dunning. Political Theories*, pp. 231 ff.

local authorities. The characteristics of different people are to be regulated by different systems of law while the king will co-ordinate all the various communities to the ultimate end of peace.

Though writers on Indian polity have often tried to find parallels between the thought of Hindu India and that of classical philosophers such as Plato and Aristotle, and while the resemblance between the *arthaśāstra* and Machiavelli's *Prince* has perhaps been overstressed, we feel that the general attitude to politics of the writers of our period is perhaps closer to that of Dante than to that of any earlier or later Western political theorist. Perhaps it is possible to account for this by general similarities of political conditions. Both Mediaeval Italy and Mediaeval India were parcelled out into many small territories, which were constantly at war with one another. In both Italy and India there were recollections of a great empire which had existed in earlier days, and had bestowed peace and security on its citizens, in Italy the memory of Rome, in India of the Guptas, remembered in the legends of Vikramāditya. Both in Italy and India religion claimed the greater share of the loyalty of the people (though in India religion was not organised under a single head), and in both lands the king's function was thought to be subordinated to religious purposes, and the king, for all his divine appointment, to be in reality humbler in the scale of values than the priest (though probably the stronger Popes and great religious dignitaries of the Mediaeval West had more political power simply by virtue of their offices than any Indian brāhmaṇa). Both Europe and India had a system of government involving delegation of power by the king to subordinate kings and chiefs the system called feudal in Europe, and which may loosely be called feudal in India.

Dante, and Machiavelli after him, advocated a strong conquering monarch who would 'please the people', and at the same time bring most of Italy under a single government. Here they fundamentally agree with the Indian Political theorists. And as in Italy so in India such a monarch did not appear, and many centuries were to pass before either land was again unified. Italy became a prey to invading armies from Germany, France and Spain, India was overrun by the Muslim Turks.

During the days of the declining glory of India, though its rulers often tried to maintain the policies laid down in the literature on the subject, they were far removed from the people and failed to meet the needs of the time and understand their own weaknesses. Consequently, when the waves of the Muslim invasion arrived they could not face them, and were forced to accept foreign domination.

The Muslims had not only the superior military strength but better political ideologies as well. The divine origin and the divinity of the Hindu kings established the superiority of one over many. It localised the office of kingship in certain families, and the people had no say in the appointment of their ruler. Kingship was hereditary, and the throne was usually occupied according to the law of primogeniture. There is a good deal of difference between this and the Muslim concept of sovereignty. According to orthodox Sunnī[1] theory sovereignty lay in the Muslim brotherhood under God, and this might confer sovereignty on any bonafide Muslim. There is no doubt that Muslims ceased to elect their rulers in the course of time, and the new caliph was usually nominated by the retiring caliph. But this nomination of the new caliph was to be approved by the leading court officials and the other important men in the state, who were responsible for his election, and the elective theory[2] had not lost its importance entirely. Thus the fact that the approval of the court officials was required before a ruler could come to the throne marks a certain popular character in Muslim sovereignty which was lacking in Hindu kingship.

Another important feature of Muslim sovereignty was equality before law. The Caliph stood on same footing as his humble subjects. It has been observed by Gibb and Bowen[3] that "a caliph guilty of immorality or grave heresy thereby violated the 'contract' which he was held to have made with the electors and became deserving of deposition". This doctrine was maintained because the interpretation of the

1. *Some Aspects of Muslim Administration*, p. 2.
2. *Ibid.*
3. *Islamic Society and the West*. p. 28.

Islamic law was vested in the body of the *Ulemā* or students of the spiritual legacy of Muhammad.[1] We are told that many of the Abbasid Caliphs of Iraq tried to gain authority over the law, but the *Ulemā* were successful in maintaining their prerogatives. On the other hand the case was different with the Hindus. Hindus had formulated an unequal law and placed the king at the head of justice, as we have considered earlier. Hindu kings[2], being the founts of justice, often tended to look after their own interests first and only then tried to maintain justice in the kingdom as we have seen in the case of Candrāpīda[3] and other kings. This must have removed the Hindu kings far from their people, and helped to lead to the downfall of the Hindu sovereignty.

We have considered earlier that many of the Hindu kings failed to perform their duties, but they continued to rule in pomp and glory because they had none to stop their autocratic rule. Theoreticians like Śukra[4] stated that the rule of even a vicious king should be tolerated. Nārada[5] stated that the people like a wife should respect and obey the command of even a worthless king. Thus instead of overthrowing a bad king the people were taught to tolerate his tyrannical rule. On the other hand the caliph did not enjoy his prestige and power by any inherent rights of his own. The source of his political power was in the Muslim community. It is true that the Muslim law enjoins the Muslim to obey the Caliph almost implicitly, but the obedience is not entirely unqualified. In cases of disregard of the Islamic law and of failure to discharge his responsibility he ran the risk of forfeiting all claims to obedience. The approval of the court-officials at the time of the enthronement of the Caliph offered a loop-hole for avoiding an undesirable caliph and kept alive the ultimate sovereignty of the Muslim people. Though there are not many examples of actual rebellion yet the ultimate sovereignty of the people would have hung like the sword of

1. Ibid, p. 26.
2. *Supra*. p.
3. Supra. p.
4. Supra. p.
5. Ibid.

Damocles over the caliph's head and restrained him to some extent[1].

Moreover one of the most important factors leading to the Muslim success in India was the indivisibility of Muslim sovereignty. According to the Muslim doctrine the caliph was the supreme authority of the kingdom. Nobody on earth could share his sovereign rights. The majority of the orthodox jurists recognised only one caliph. There could not be two caliphs at one and the same time. No doubt provision was made for two caliphs, but only when a wide sea separated two countries.[2] Even though from the time of the middle of the tenth century A.D. *de facto* power was exercised by independent governors, jurists like Al-Mavādī, who were in the service of sultans, insisted that lesser rulers held their power by delegation from the one legitimate Abbasid Caliph. But the case was totally different with the Hindus. The whole country was divided into several petty principalities which we have enumerated in our introduction. These Hindu chiefs were completely independent and lacked any sense of solidarity. Thus they weakened the defence of the country and encouraged the Muslims to invade India.

These are a few possible reasons that may have established the superiority of the Muslims over the Hindus. The Muslims fought with vigour for their sovereign and died with a zeal to establish their ideology. On the other hand the Hindus, proud of their power but torn by mutual enmity and corruption, failed to resist the invasion and gave way to Islam in India.

1. *Some Aspects of Muslim Administration*, pp. 5 ff.
2. Ibid., p. 6.

BIBLIOGRAPHY

A. Texts in Indian Languages and Translation.

Abhilaṣitārtha Cintāmaṇi, Ed. R. Shama Shastri Mysore, 1926.

Ācārāṅga Sūtra, tr. H. Jacobi in S. B. E., vol xxii, Oxford, 1884.

Agni Purāṇa, Ed. Rājendra Lall Mitra, Calcutta, 1876.

Agni Purāṇa, Ānandāśrama Series, Ed. H. N. Āpte, 1900.

Agni Purāṇa, tr. M. N. Dutta, Calcutta, 1904.

Aitareya Brāhmaṇa, Ed. and tr. Prof. M. Haug, Bombay, 1863.

Amarakoṣa, Ed. H. Shastri, Benares, 1937.

Aparājitapṛcchā, Ed. B. Bhaṭṭācārya, Gaekwad Oriental Institute, Baroda, 1950.

Bhāṭṭadīpikā, Ed, C. Tārālaṅkāra, Calcutta, 1899.

Bhaviṣyatkathā of Dhanapāla, Ed. C.D. Dala, Baroda, 1923.

Bṛhaspati Arthaśāstra, Ed. F. W. Thomas, The Punjab Sanskrit Book Depot, Lahore, 1921.

Bṛhaspatismṛti, tr. J. Jolly, Sacred Books of the East, vol. xxxiii, Oxford, 1889.

Campū Rāmāyaṇa of Bhoja Rāja, Ed. J. Vidyāsāgara, Calcutta, 1878.

Dīgha Nikāya, vol. iii, Ed. T. G. W. Rhys David, London, 1932.

Gautamasmṛti, tr. G. Bühler, Sacred Books of the East. Oxford, 1839.

Hammīra Mahākāvya of Nayacandra Sūri, Bombay, 1879.

Harṣacarita of Bāṇa, Ed. R.P. Parab, Bombay, 1925.

Harṣacarita of Bāṇa, tr. E.B. Cowell and F.W. Thomas, London, 1897.

Harivaṃśa Purāṇa of Jinasena Sūri, Ed. Dharilal, Manika Lall Digambar Jaina Granthamala Samiti, Bombay, 1930.

Jaiminīya-Nyāyamālā-Vistara, Ed. E.B. Cowell, London, 1878.

Kādambarī of Bāṇa, tr. C.M. Ridding, London, 1896.

Kāmandakīyanītisāra, Ed. J. Vidyāsāgara, Calcutta, 1875.

Kāmandakīyanītisāra. tr. M.N. Dutt, Calcutta, 1896.

Kathāsaritsāgara, Ed. Durgā Prasād and K.P. Parab, Bombay, 1930.

Kathāsaritsāgara. Tr. C.H. Tawney, 2 vols. Calcutta, 1880-1884.

Kātyāyanasmṛti, Ed. P V. Cane, Poona, 1933.

Kauṭilīya Arthaśāstra, Ed. and tr. R. Shama Sastri, Mysore, 1924.

Kṛtyakalpataru of Lakṣmīdhara, vol. xi, Ed. K.V. Rangasvami Aiyangar, Baroda, 1943.

Kumārapālacarita of Hemacandra, Ed. P.L, Vaidya, Poona, 1936.

Laghvarhannīti of Hemacandra, Ed. Ahmadabad, 1906.

Liṅgapurāṇa, Ed. Kṣemarāja, Bombay.

Mahābhārata, Critical Edition, Ed V.S. Sukthanker and others, Poona, 1927 (in progress)

Mahābhārata, Ed. P.C. Roy, Calcutta, Saka Sambat, 1810.

Mahābhārata, Tr. P.C. Roy, Calcutta, 1884-96.

Mahā Purāṇa, Ed. Panna Lall Jaina, Kashi, 1951.

Mānasollāsa of king Someśvara, Ed. Śri Gondekar, Baroda, 1939.

Manusmṛti with Medhātithi's Commentary, Ed. G. Jha, Calcutta, 1939.

Manusmṛti with Medhātithi's Commentary, Tr. G. Jha, Calcutta, 1924.

Mārkaṇḍeya Purāṇa, Ed. Rev. K.M. Banerjee, Calcutta, 1862.

Mārkaṇḍeya Purāṇa, Tr. M.N. Dutta, Calcutta, 1896.

Matsya Purāṇa, Ed. H.N. Āpte, Ānandāśrama Series, 1907.

Matsya Purāṇa, Sacred Books of the Hindus, vol. vviii, Allahabad, 1916.

Mīmāṃsādarśanaṃ of Śabarasvāmi, Ed. Ratna Gopāla, Bhaṭṭa, Benares, 1910.

Nāgānanda of Harṣa, Ed. R. D. Karmarkar, 3rd. Ed., Poona, 1953.

Nāradasmṛti, Tr. J. Jolly, Oxfort, 1889.

Nītivākyāmṛta of Somadeva, Published by Manikchandra Digambara Jaina, Granthamala, 1989 V.S.

Prabandhacintāmaṇi cf Merutuṅgācārya, Ed. Jina Vijaya Muni, Shantiniketan, 1933.

Prabandhacintāmaṇi of Merutuṅgācārya, Hindi tr. Hazari Prasad Dvivedi, Shantiniketan, 1940.

The Pṛthvirāj Rāso of Chand Bardai, Ed. Syam Sundar Das, Benares, 1904.

Priyadarśikā of Harṣa, Ed. and tr. G. K. Nariman, A.V.W. Jackson and C.J. Ogden, Columbia University Press, 1923.

Rājadharmakaustubha of Anantadeva, Ed. Kamala Pṛṣṇa Smṛtitīrtha, 1935.

Rājanītiratnākara of Caṇḍeśvara, Ed. K.P. Jayaswal, 2nd Ed., Patna, 1936.

Rājataraṅgiṇī of Kalhaṇa, Ed. M.A. Stein, Bombay, 1892.

Rājataraṅgiṇī of Kalhaṇa, tr. M.A. Stein, 2 vols., London, 1900.

Rāmacarita of Sandhyākara Nandin, Ed. and tr. R.C. Majumder, Rajshahi, 1939.

Śukranītisāra, Ed. Gustav Oppert, Madras, 1882.

Śukranītisāra, tr. B.K. Sarkar, Allahabad, 1914.

Suvarṇabhāsottama Sūtra, Ed. Johannes Nobel, Leipzig, 1937.

Suvarṇaprabhāsa Sūtra, Ed. Bunyiu Nanjio, Kyoto, 1931.

Triṣaṣṭiśalākāpuruṣacarita of Hemacandra, Bhavanagar, 1906.

Uttara-Rāma-Carita of Bhavabhūti, Nirṇaya Sāgar Press, Bombay, 1949.

Uttara-Rāma-Carita of Bhavabhūti, tr. C.H. Tawney, Calcuuta, 1874.

Utttara-Rām-Carita of Bhavabhūti, Hindi tr. Ramdas and Vireshvar Nath, 2nd Ed., Benares, V.S. 1992.

Vaśiṣṭhasmṛti, tr. G. Bühler, S. B. E. vol. xiv, Oxford, 1882.

Vikramāṅkadevacarita of Vidyāpati Bilhaṇa, Ed. G. Bühler 1875.

Yājñavalkyasmṛti with Aparārka's Commentary, Ānandāśrama Series, 1903.

Yuktikalpataru of Bhoja, Ed. Isvara Chandra Sāstri, Calcutta, 1917.

B. Foreign Accounts

Alberuni's India, tr. Dr. Edward C. Sachau, 2 vols. London, 1888.

Ancient India, As described by Megasthenes and Arrian, tr. J.W. McCrindle, and. Ed., Calcutta, 1926.

Buddhist Records of the Western World of Si-yu-ki, tr. S. Beal, 2 vols., London, 1883.

Diodorus Siculus, Loeb Classical Series, London, 1933.

Fa-Hsian's record of the Buddhist Kingdoms, by J. Legge, Oxford, 1886.

Life of Hiuen Tsiang, Tr. S. Beal, London, 1911.

On Yuan Chwang's Travels in India, by T. Watters, 2 vols. London, 1904-5.

C. Archaeological Sources

Antiquities of Chamba, vol. i, Ed. J. Ph. Vogel, Calcutta, 1911.

Epigraphia Indica, Calcutta.

Indian Antiquary, Bombay.

South Indian Epigraphic Reports, Madras.

Secondary Sources A.

Advanced History of India, by R. C. Majumder, H.C. Raychoudhuri and K.K. Dutta, London, 1948.

Age of Imperial Kanauj (History and Culture of the Indian People, vol. iv), Ed. R.C. Majumder, Bombay, 1955.

The Agrarian System in Ancient India, by U.N. Ghoshal, Calcutta, 1930.

Ancient History of Saurāṣṭra, by K. J. Virji, Bombay, 1955.

Aspects of Ancient Indian Polity, by N.N. Law, Oxford, 1921.

Aspects of Political Ideas and Institutions in Ancient India, by R. S. Sharma, Published by Motilal Banarsi Das 1959.

The Beginning of Indian Historiography, by U.N. Ghoshal, Calcutta, 1944.

The Caliphate, by T. W. Arnold, Oxford, I924.

Cambridge History of India, vol. iii, Ed. Sir W. Haig, Cambridge, 1928.

Caulukyas of Gujarat, by A. K. Majumder, Bombay, 1956.
Church, State and Society, by Gerd Tellembach, Oxford, 1948.
The Commerce between the Roman Empire and India by E.H. Warmington, Cambridge, 1928.
Contributions to the History of the Hindu Revenue System, by U.N. Ghoshal, Calcutta, 1929.
Corporate Life in Ancient India, by R.C. Majumder, Calcutta, 1922.
The Divine Rights of Kings, by J. N. Figgis, Cambridge, 1896.
Downfall of Hindu India (C. 1000 to 1200 A.D.) by C.V. Vaidya, Poona, 1926.
The Dynastic History of Northern India (Early Mediaeval period), by H.C. Ray, Calcutta, 1936.
The Economic Life in Northern India, by Lallanji Gopal
Early History of India, by V.A. Smith, 3rd Ed., Oxford, 1914.
Elements of Political Science, by S. Leacock, London, 1911.
The Glory that was Gurjaradeśa, Part iii, by K.M. Munshi, Bombay 1948.
Golden Bough, vol. i, by Sir James Frazer, London, 1911.
A Grammar of Politics, by H. J. Laski, London, 1951.
Das Grundeigentum in Indien, Kauṭalīya-Studien I, by B. Breloer, Bonn, 1927.
Hindu Administrative Institutions, by V. R. R. Dikshitar, Madras, 1929.
Hindu Polity by K. P. Jayaswal, Banglore, 1955.
History of Dharmaśāstra, by P. V. Kane, 4 vols. Poona, 1930-53.
History of Hindu Political Theories, by U.N. Ghoshal, Oxford University Press, 1923.
The History of India As Told by Its Own Historians, by H. M. Elliot & J. Dowson, vol. 1-3, London 1867, 1869, 1871.
History of Indian Shipping, by R. K. Mukherjee, Bombay, 1912.
History of Kanauj, by R.S. Tripathi, Benares, 1937.
Ideologies of War and Peace in Ancient India by Indra

International Law and Inter-State Relations in Ancient India, by Hiralal Chatterjee, Firma K. L. Mukhopadhyay, 1958.

International Law in Ancient India, by S. V. Vishwanath, Bombay, 1925.

Inter-State Relations in Ancient India, by N. N. Law, Calcutta, 1920.

An Introduction to Politics, by H. J. Laski, London, 1954.

Islamic Society and the West, by H. A. R. Gibb and H. Bowen, London, 1950.

Kingship, by A. M. Hocart, London, 1927.

Kingship and Law, by F. Kern, Oxford, 1948.

Life of Hemacandrācārya, by G. Bühler, tr. M. Patel, Shantiniketan, 1936.

Megasthenes en de Indische Maatschappij, by B. C. J. Timmer, Amsterdam, 1930.

Monarchy and Three Political Letters of Dante, tr. Donald D. Nicholl, London, 1954.

A History of Indian Political Ideas, by U.N. Ghoshal, Oxford University, Press, 1959.

A History of Political Theories, Ancient and Medieval, W. A Dunning, New York, 1951.

Origin and Evolution of Kingship by K. M. Panikkar, 1938 Edition.

Politics of Aristotle, tr. William Ellis, Everyman's Library Series, 1952.

The Position of Women in Hindu Civilisation, by A. S. Altekar, Benares, 1938.

Positive Background of Hindu Sociology, by B. K. Sarkar, Allahabad, 1914.

The Prince of Nicolo Machiavelli, Tr. W.K. Marriot, Everyman's Libray Herts. 1952.

Public Administration in Ancient India, by Pramatha Nath Banerjee, London, 1916.

Rājadharma, by K. V. Rangasvami Aiyangar, Madras, 1949.

Republic of Plato, Tr. H. D. P. Lee, The Penguin Classics, London, 1955.

Republic of Plato, Tr. Paul Shorey, Loeb Classical Series, London, 1935.

Social-Contract, by Locke, Hume & Rouseau, The World's Classics, London, 1956.

The Social Organization in North East India in Buddha's Time, by Richard Fick, Tr. S. K. Maitra, Calcutta, 1920.

Some Aspects of Ancient Indian Polity, by K. V. Rangasvami, Aiyangar, Madras, 1935.

Some Aspects of Hindu Polity, by D. R. Bhandarkar Benares, 1929.

Some Aspects of the Hindu View of Life According to Dharmaśāstra, by K. V. Rangasvami Aiyanger, Baroda, 1952.

Some Aspects of Muslim Administration, by R. P. Tripathi, Allahabad, 1936.

South Indian Polity, by T. V. Mahalingam, Madras, 1955.

Sovereignty in Ancient India, by H. N. Sinha, London, 1938.

State and Government in Ancient India, by A. S. Altekar, Benares, 1949.

The State in Ancient India, by Beni Prasad, Allahabad 1928.

The Substance of Politics, by A. Appadorai, 6th Ed., Madras, 1952.

The Vākāṭaka-Gupta Age, by A.S. Altekar and R. C. Majumder, Baneras, 1954.

The White Umbrella, by M. Brown, University of Columbia Press, 1953.

The Wonder that was India, by A. L. Basham, London, 1954.

Journals

Annals of the Bhandarkar Oriental Research Institute, Poona.

Annals of the Oriental Research, University of Madras, Madras.

Bharatiya Vidya, Bharatiya Vidya Bhavan, Bombay.

Bulletin of the School of Oriental and African Studies, London.

Harvard Journal of Asian Studies, Cambridge, U.S.A.

Indian Culture, Calcutta.

Indian Historical Quarterly, Calcutta.

Journal of the American Oriental Socienty, New Haven.

Journal of the Andhra Historical Society, Rājahmundry.

Journal of the Annamalai University, Annamalai Nagar.

Journal of the Assam Research Society, Gauhati.
Journal of the Bengal Asiatic Society, Calcutta.
Journal of the Bihar and Orissa Research Society, Bankipure.
Journal of the Bombay Branch of the Royal Asiatic Society, Bombay.
Journal of the Department of Letters, Calcutta University.
Journal of the East India Association, London.
Journal of Indian History, Trivandrum.
Journal of the Royal Asiatic Society, London.
Sir Āsutosh Silver Jubilee Volume, Calcutta, 1925.

INDEX